THE MATRIARCH

THE MATRIARCH

A story about my grandmother

Eileen McNeal

To order additional copies of this book, contact:
Xlibris Corporation
1-888-795-4274
www.Xlibris.com
Orders@Xlibris.com
65183

CONTENTS

ACKNOWLEDGEMENTS

Thanks to my brother Wesley Cherry, Uncle Dick and Aunt Rebecca Calloway. I also thank my dear sister Marjorie Reed and loving brother Charles (Skeeter) Cherry who have gone on now as others in this book to heaven. Their excellent memories and total recall has made this book as accurate as I could make it. Thanks also to my daughter Valerie Martinenko and my son Mark McNeal for their encouragement, but most of all thanks to my son Michael McNeal who had to listen to every chapter as it was written and give me his honest opinion.

THE MATRIARCH

I see now that she kept us all together Like beads upon a string, both large and small The multi-colored necklace of her years We all were precious to her fingers whether of glass or gold, in us she held her all of living, her sum of laughter, love and tears.

And loving her we understood each other in dim awareness of the pattern wrought by her, the matriarch, that slender thread unseen yet bound us one unto another With pride at heritage Must we be caught less closely now when she we loved is gone

Discovered by Marjorie Reed from a McCalls Magazine 1941
by Grace Maddock Miller

MARRIAGE LICENSE BUREAU

IN THE COURT OF COMMON PLEAS OF NORTHAMPTON COUNTY ORPHANS' COURT DIVISION

STATE OF PENNSYLVANIA
COUNTY OF NORTHAMPTON, SS.

CERTIFICATE OF THE MARRIAGE OF

LEVI MILLS

and

LOGAINA ARMSTEAD

I, **DOROTHY L. COLE**, Clerk of the Orphans' Court, Division of the Court of Common Pleas, Northampton County, Pennsylvania, being also the Marriage License Clerk of the said County, do hereby certify and make known:-

That __LEVI MILLS__   __EASTON, PA__   __11/25/1872__
    name   residing at   age/date of birth

and __LOGAINA ARMSTEAD__   __208 SPRING GARDEN STREET   EASTON,PA__   __3/1880__
    name   residing at   age/date of birth

were united in Marriage on the __1ST__ day of __OCTOBER__, 19_01_,

at __EASTON__, Pennsylvania by __H.B. RANKIN__
                                  Minister of the Gospel/District Justice

in accordance with Marriage License Number __9475__ duly issued by the Clerk

of said Court, as appears, of record in Marriage License Docket No. __11__,

Page __517__, reference thereunto being had will more fully and at large

appear.

IN WITNESS WHEREOF, I have hereunto set my hand and affixed the seal of said

Court at Easton, Pennsylvania, this __29TH__ day of __MARCH__ __2000__.

Dorothy L. Cole
_____
Clerk of the Orphans' Court
Division of the Court of Common Pleas

My Grandmother's
wedding license

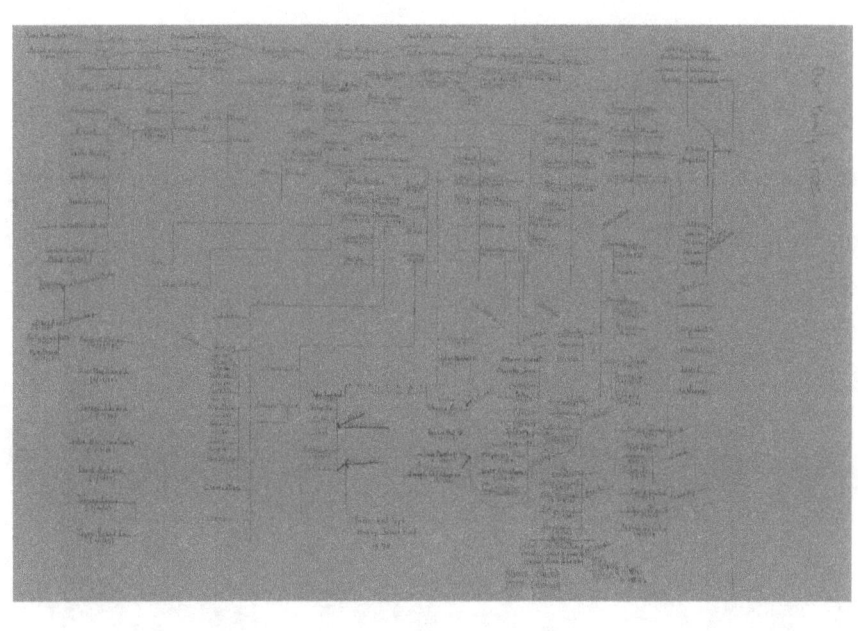

The Millennium is looming over the horizon and while some of humanity is frantically stocking up supplies for the Y2K disaster, I begin to think about my past. There is right now at this moment, a war going on in Kosovo, children are shooting children in the schools of our nation, and the president of our country has just narrowly missed impeachment In this same period though, wives are having their deceased husbands children, we can see our baby's face before it is born, and we can find anything on the Internet we want to know providing we have a layman's knowledge of the computer.

Yes, we are on the brink of exciting new discoveries of, I have no doubt, there will be many. Who, though, am I? What has made me the way I am? What type of experiences did my ancestors have during the years before my birth? In my search to find out many things, some of them sad, some of them wonderful, but nevertheless all exciting which I will attempt to put down on the pages that follow.

CHAPTER 1

Logania

My grandmother Logania was born in the year 1881 in Virginia. Although this was sixteen long years after the thirteenth amendment which freed the slaves, my grandmother grew up in a time of turmoil and violence towards people of color. Despite the obvious oppressions and difficulties, our family suffered for the sole transgression of being black, we have persevered and even surpassed all expectations. I don't claim to know the exact story of my ancestors but I can presume to understand some of what they felt and learned and write the story of how I think it happened.

"Logania. Logania, get up and help your brothers and sisters get ready for church. Hurry now," Ardelia called.

Then she turned back to the smoldering job of frying bacon over an open fireplace on a hot July morning. The babies Pearl and Bessie and little Kelia were all whining for their breakfast. They crawled around the dirt floor of the tiny cabin whimpering for their mother. Ardelia wrapped the bright red scarf more tightly around her short, dark, curls. It was already damp with sweat.

"Mary Lou," she called, "Please get up and feed the babies. The chickens ain't been fed yet and old Bessie ain't going to give us no more milk if you don't give her some hay." Young Logania climbed out of bed and dressed swiftly. Through the open window, a warm breeze ruffled her long, brown curls as she nudged her brothers awake. George, who they all called Wash, named after the famous general, grumbled and moaned but finally stumbled to his feet rubbing his eyes. Sunday morning was the only day Wash didn't have to go to the fields. He sure wanted to sleep. Every morning except Sunday, as soon as the sun smiled it's first grin from the heavens, old Harry would pick up the boys in the old farm wagon and take them to the wheat fields. Papa Harry and the other men would scythe and cradle the wheat. Then Ma and all the women would rake and bind. Then Wash and his two younger brothers stacked the wheat. The girls stacked too, under the hot Virginia sun. Only the smallest were exempted from the grueling work, and they were placed somewhere near, in the shade where their mother could keep a careful eye on them. Ardelia fashioned a sort of sack on her back which carried the little one with her as she worked and kept her out of danger. So on Sunday, the one morning they could rest, Wash wanted only to sleep. Ardelia wouldn't hear of it.

"Get your body to church, Wash and worship the Lord. One day he gonna give you fields of your own to farm. Then you be in charge." Wash got up then, but secretly he thought, if that was gonna be the Lord's gift, more work, he rather stay in bed. The smoky smell of frying bacon wafted to the loft, along with their mother's voice, more shrill now calling for Mary Lou to get the baby.

Tiredly Ardelia set two small bowls of grits on the table and then tied little Bessie and Kelia to the old wooden kitchen chairs to eat their breakfast. Mary Lou fed the baby milk, as one by one the others stumbled into the yard, to splash chilly pump water over their faces and hands, and then back to the table for a quick breakfast of bacon and huge bowls of grits swimming in butter.

Her younger sister Nannie was deathly afraid of the chickens which pecked in the front yard waiting for their breakfast, so Logania had this job too, in addition to helping the younger ones plait their hair for church. After feeding the chickens and avoiding Sarah, the mean old hen, who always pecked viciously at her heels, she went to the pasture to get old Peyton, their one and only horse. Then she and her three sisters all piled on Peyton, and her brothers Robert and Wash walked along side. Charles, the youngest brother stayed home as he was not as strong as his brothers and sisters and Ma always let him rest on Sunday.

Logania loved this walk every Sunday. Through the woods they followed the path, the sounds of birds twittering overhead, the rhythmic plop of Peyton's feet as he plodded along. She loved to watch the squirrels and field mice scattering as they approached, and inhale the earthy smell of the woods. Wind shifted the branches overhead, causing the leaves to make mysterious, twisting, patterns on the ground. Her two brothers shoved each other and tussled playfully along the way and then suddenly, they were out of the woods facing the clearing where sat the church.

A tiny church it was, all whitewashed so it gleamed in the morning sun. Emerald green vines twined and twisted themselves around the walls and perched on the steeple sat a huge golden cross. Huge oak trees surrounded the sides and a tiny sign out front professed it to be The Oak Union Baptist Church.

Through the open windows, the most beautiful music was playing. Someone played Just A Little Walk With Jesus on the piano to welcome the congregation. Logania and her sisters hurried in to find their favorite wooden bench, while Robert and Wash tied up Peyton. The church was just as small inside as out and it filled up quickly. Logania and Mary Lou loved to sing the old hymns and listen to the choir sing. They were always a little nervous when the minister spoke, but they enjoyed that too.

When the collection plate came around, Logania untied her crisp, white handkerchief in which Ma had placed two nickels for them to give. It seemed a lot to part with, as they were so poor, but she proudly deposited it into the

The Oak Union Baptist Church

plate, shyly smiling at the deacon as he moved on to the next row. The children enjoyed this time in church, as living on a farm as they did, this was one of the few respites from work they had. So it was with some disappointment, they realized the benediction was being said and it was time to return home.

Sunday afternoon at the Armstead household was a busy time. Ardelia had to wash all the clothes the family wore all week and patch anything that was fixable. Ardelia heated over the open fireplace the old buck tub full of strong lye soap. She mixed the boiling clothes with an old stick to get out most of the dirt. In the hot July afternoon, the steam alone made the heat excruciating in the little hut. Then Ardelia took a round log and rolled the clothes around it to wring out as much water as she could. Then she stretched them out in the hot July sun to dry.

The girls she sent to the garden to hoe and pull the vines that choked and smothered any vegetable brave enough to grow. The smaller ones sat in the shade of the huge oak tree and played with the rag dolls their momma had made them. Little Kelia blew on his whistle as Pa didn't allow him to play with dolls. Pa rounded up the boys to go fishing. They marched off down the road their bare feet slapping against the ground singing we'se a going to the fishing hole, fishing hole, to catch a mess of catfish.

Round about the time Ardelia got the clothes stretched out in the sun, the girls returned from the garden with the vegetables they picked. Mary Lou carried a basket of green beans and tomatoes. Logania picked a few cabbages and Nannie even found a small watermelon just at the right stage for eating. Ardelia set all the girls to peeling and washing, and Mary Lou put the youngest down to take a nap. Just about the time the beans were done, Harry and the boys returned.

We caught more than Pa, we caught more than Pa, the boys were singing as they trotted up the path.

Ardelia came to the door with her hands on her hips. "What's this yammering I hear?", she asked. "How'd you do Robert, Charles, Wash? Let's see them fish you caught."

"Ma, I caught two, and so did Robert and Wash, but Pa, he only caught one," Charles said timidly.

"Well, where is Pa?" asked Ardelia.

"He said he was checking on Peyton," piped up Robert, "but I think he's hiding from you, Ma."

"Is that so?" Ardelia asked smiling. "Well then you take Pa's one little fish and you and Wash take them fish out back and clean em for cookin. I got the coals just right for frying up some catfish."

"Ahhh Ma," grumbled Robert, he and his brothers went toting their catch of fish. Soon the sound of sizzling fish and the tantalizing, smoky smell had everyone leaving their chores and scrambling to the small kitchen for supper. When supper was over, the girls cleaned the table and washed up with a lot of squabbling over who was to do what.

Ardelia had been a slave when she was a young girl and worked in the big house kitchen. She'd grown up watching the other slaves keep that kitchen spic and span clean and though she lived in a cramped little cabin, it belonged to her and she was adamant about keeping it clean. The hard dirt floor had to be swept every day. The dishes had to be rinsed off after every meal and all the garbage had to be buried every day. Some things Ardelia used to fertilize her garden.

She remembered the slave days well, and told her daughters stories of how when they'd lived on the master's plantation, the slaves had strewn garbage around on purpose to keep the master away and insure a little privacy.

"Of course, none of us liked living like that," Ardelia stated angrily, "But it was one of the few things we had control over. Don't you never let nobody tell you we dirty cause we not. And that's why I better never see a speck of dirt round here."

Then her voice got real soft and she smile sort of wistful like and say "on Sunday mornings your Pa, Harry, would come a courting me when the master's family went to church. Harry would talk that old cook Annie on his plantation into giving him some fresh baked biscuits. Then he'd bring those biscuits to me straight-away. We had a special place behind the slave quarters where we'd sit and gobble up them biscuits. I can still member the taste of those buttery tasting things. Lord, but they was good. Then we'd talk about our future. Martha was already born then, but things was in a terrible way. They was fixing to go to war."

Always at this point Logania asked, "How did you meet, Pa, Mama?"

And Mary Lou say, "Yes, Mama tell us how."

"Well, Miss Martha, my mistress took a liking to me. She took me into the big house and taught me how to sew and cook. She saw how the slaves always be running away and getting whipped and sometimes even worse than that. She tell me many a time. she thought I very intelligent, so I think she worry I try to run away too, and get caught, maybe be killed or something, so though I only be thirteen, she brought Harry from the next plantation to meet me and we took to each other right away. I think she figure if I have a passel of young uns and a man I stay put and out of harm's way. That Martha was a right smart woman, which is why I name our first baby Martha.

"But Mama, didn't you want to run away?, Logania asked.

"You're always the logical one, Logania," Ardelia said with a smile. "Of course, I want to be free Honey, but I see other families sold away from each other. I see slaves beaten every day just for stealing a piece of bread. I hear stories about slaves being tortured on other plantations."

"Oh Mama", Nannie whispered. "That's terrible."

"Lord, yes, Honey. That's why I tell my girls and my sons too. Be strong and think. Sometimes you get out of some bad times if you just think. I learn to accept my life, Nannie, but I could hope for a better life, and now I have hopes for you all to have an even better life."

Ardelia sent the girls off to do their chores. As she rocked little Pearl, she thought back to her grandmother's time when some Negro named Nat Turner had organized a rebellion. Fifty-five white Virginians had been brutally killed and the whites had panicked. They'd questioned Negroes and killed many who didn't give the right answers or have passes to show. Ardelia knew things hadn't changed much. She'd worried constantly that Harry would be shot when he sneaked over to her farm to visit at night.

"Delia, Honey, yo don't have to worry", he'd say. I know how to take care of myself. I'se workin right now on building a church with a bunch of other Negroes. And when they pays me for de work, I'm gonna buy you and me and baby Martha free."

"Ardelia would just smile sort of wistful like. Then she say, "that be real nice, Harry, real nice."

Harry never got to finish working on the church as the mistreatment of the slaves exploded into a bloody war between The North and The South. For several years Harry followed his master from battle to battle and carried wounded back from the war zones. His chores included polishing his master's boots, and the harnesses, and cleaning the rifles. Master O'Brien had never liked the idea of owning slaves too much, he went to war, but his heart wasn't into fighting, so though he never let on, he was just as relieved as the slaves when the war ended.

After the war, the slaves were officially free men but most of them were confused with their status. They were still treated as slaves but yet free to pursue their own futures without any guidance, sort of like a boat floating downstream through an obstacle course without a rudder. Harry, though, never faltered. he continued working for his old master, now for wages, and begged a few acres of land that he could plant his own tobacco crop on. When he'd saved a little money, he bought the old cabin nearest his plot of land and moved Ardelia and Martha, who was now almost ten years old into it. Ardelia, right away, christened their new home with a son who they named George Washington but everyone called the little guy Wash, for short. There were no more long breaks between children as there were during the war. Ardelia had a child just about every three years until she had her last child, little Pearl at the age of forty-four.

During this time Ardelia and Harry worked hard to bring their brood up right. Ardelia had an old speller that Mistress Martha had secretly given her when she left the plantation. On cold, winter nights, Ardelia would struggle to learn the words in the speller so that she could teach her children, but she had little success. Each of the children would attempt from time to time to learn a few words, but with no real teacher around, they learned very little.

One blustery, cold night all the children gathered close to the fire, the only warm spot in the little cabin. The younger ones Kay, Bessie, and little Pearl were tucked cozily into bed. Wash and Pa were out in the frigid night making sure all the animals had food and water. Their older sister Martha lived up the road apiece with her husband, Henry Wilson and was expecting her first child. Ardelia, who was feeling poorly, due to bad cold that lingered on, wrapped herself up in a heavy blanket and sat down in front of the fire, in the only chair with goose down cushions.

"Ma, why do we have to study so much?" Nannie asked. "We are just farm girls. We're all going to marry like Martha and have little ones. We don't need no schoolin for that."

In the silence that followed, sleet rattled like tiny claws against the roof. The wind whistled about the cabin causing the candles to gyrate wildly producing ominous shapes that moved and writhed on the cabin walls.

Nannie shuddered.

"Come here, Nannie," called Ardelia gently. She pulled Nannie on to her lap.

"First off, I want you to talk better than me. I wants people to say those Armstead children are so smart. I want all my kin to get the best book learning they can get. Come close and I'll tell you why. I'm gonna tell you the story of your stepmother Vinie Nightengale Fegan."

"My Pa married my Ma in 1837 but it was one of those matches that just didn't work. Ma said he stayed around until I was born, but though he loved me, his Ardelia, his eye was set on someone else. Her name was Angeline and Ma said she was a looker. The other slaves whispered about her Pa being the white master and everyone knew it to be true, but he never owned up to it. Anyway she was real fair and had long reddish hair. She wore it swinging free and ran about doing as little work as possible. My Pa had a powerful desire for her, so one day he just up and took off and Ma hears later that he married Angeline and is living on her plantation now. Pa and Angeline were true in love. Angeline settled down then to be a real fine wife and her and Pa had ten little ones. Pa use to bring the older two, John and Logania Elizabeth over to play with me until old Master told him not to come no more and to stay on his own plantation.'

Logania looked up startled. "Ma, you mean she was named Logania, too?"

"Sure was Honey. I thought it was a pretty name and she was one right sweet girl too, like you. That's why I named you Logania."

"But Pa wasn't allowed to visit no more. Round about that time Angeline had George Matthews. She had a hard time birthing the baby and before little George was a week old, Angeline died. The old midwife who helped her said, it weren't nobody's fault. Angeline just had too many babies too fast. My Pa was all tore up about it. He couldn't work right no more. He be out in the fields and suddenly set down and start crying. Then the overseers drag him back to the house and whip him."

"Oh Ma. Did you cry for your old Pa?" Nannie asked. "What did you do?"

"Well, Nannie, Ma knew what was goin on but she and the others kept it from me. I never knew nothin until one night Pa just up and ran away."

Mary Lou's eyes got real big. "He ran away. Oh, Ma, did he get killed?"

"No, he didn't Mary Lou. He run off into the woods. Everyone was out lookin for him. Them white folks got out the dogs to track him down. But Pa had met an Indian woman out there. Folks say she was real pretty with them long black braids and she took a liken to my Pa. She took Pa back to her camp. Her name was Viney Nightengale soon to be Fegan. my stepmother."

Robert, who'd been whittling in the corner moved closer. "Your Pa lived with the Indians, Ma? Our Pa calls em savages and he tells us to stay away from em."

"Robert, they's a lot of savages in this world and they come in all colors. At that time the savages was the slave hunters who were after my Pa, and they were gettin right angry. The story goes this Miss Nightengale sat with Pa every night teaching him to read and write. She give him Indian clothes to wear. Then she started working on a plan to get him and her up North where they can be together in peace. Once they'd mapped out the route they were traveling, Vinie talked her father Chief Thundercloud into stealing a wagon. She hooked up a couple of horses to that old wagon and by Jimmy, when they changed their clothes, they looked like two slaves on an errand for their master."

At that moment the door slammed open and Wash and Harry came in followed by a blast of cold air.

"The kettles hot, Harry," stated Ardelia. "You and Wash have some of that chicken soup. Then set down by the fire and warm yourself. I was telling the children a story about my step mother Vinie, before they go to bed."

Delia, Honey, you telling them that old Indian tale. You don't even know if it's true."

"Oh it's true enough, Harry," answered Ardelia. "Old Vinie use to tell me the story over and over when her and Pa moved back here. Course she was an old woman then, but she membered that story clear enough to tell all us young uns in the family."

"Ma, please finish the story," pleaded Logania.

"Well, I bet you can guess what they did," continued Ardelia. "Vinie used her old Master's name, Captain Wilson. She and my Pa wrote their own passes, packed some food which they hid in the back of the wagon, and then they climbed in and headed up North to Pennsylvania. Most of the time they traveled at night and hid during the day. But one morning, before they could find a good hiding place, about the time the birds start chirping, they bumped into two patrollers, who were on their way home after a night of drinking."

The tall, coarse one named Rudolph called, "hey, Sam, look a nigger and an Injun riding in a wagon. What do you think of that?"

Sam was having a hard time sitting his saddle, but he leaned forward and yelled, "just where do you all think you going?"

"My Pa was shaking like a leaf in a blizzard, but he held up his pass and said, "we got permission from Master Wilson. It's all wrote right here."

Rudolph snatched up the pass and read it. "Now why would Captain Wilson send a nigra and a Injun so far from home without supervision."

Sam rode forward and grabbed the harness. "Turn this crate around!" he said sneering. "We'll see what old Wilson has to say about this."

Then Vinie raised herself straight in that seat. "You do that," she said, "and Master Wilson's gonna be mighty angry. He's sent us to Baltimore to get lace for his daughter's wedding dress and ain't nobody else on that plantation got time to do it except us."

"Is that so?" Rudolph asked. "Why can't old Emma go pick up that lace?"

Vinie whispered soothingly to the nervous horses. Then she looked directly at Rudolph, "this here weddings gonna be a week from Saturday. Miss Emma is running all over trying to get flowers. It's a rush wedding and we was the only ones they could spare to go get the lace."

"Master Wilson knows he can trust us," chimed in Washington.

Sam looked worriedly at Rudolph. "If their telling the truth, we could cause them to cancel the wedding. Captain Wilson won't take kindly to that. With them horses, it's gonna take them a long time to get to Baltimore."

Rudolph looked up skeptically. "How you gonna buy lace? A nigger and an Injun!"

Vinie smiled slyly. "Master Wilson has written a letter," she said, and then she handed the paper to Rudolph.

Sam, who was feeling pretty sick by then said, "let em go, Rudy. If their lying we'll find out soon enough and they ain't gonna get far on them raggedy horses. Let's go."

Rudolph circled around and looked back. "If you all are lying, this is gonna be your last week on earth." Then he rode off behind Sam.

Then Vinie and my Pa near rode those horses to death, trying to get to Pennsylvania," continued Ardelia.

"Oh, Ma, did they make it? Did they?" asked Mary Lou.

"You know they did, silly" answered Logania, or Ma wouldn't be telling us the story. She never tells us any stories with a sad ending."

"You sure are right, Honey," Ardelia replied. "Pa and Viney made it safely to Pennsylvania where they settled and lived happily for many years."

"Did those old patrollers chase after em?" asked Robert.

Harry, who'd been puffing on his pipe sitting quietly at the table got up and stretched.

"No, Robert, they didn't chase em," he growled. "What Ma hasn't tole you is that all this happened after we'd been freed. Them two rednecks shouldn't have even stopped em because we was all just as free as birds."

"Now, Harry, calm down," said Ardelia quietly. "Your Pa's right though. The War Between The North And South was over and all the slaves was free, but a lot of them didn't know it, and them white folks sure didn't tell em. But Viney had been free a long time and my Pa had run away before the war so they knew they were free, war or no war. Now scoot on to bed, all of ya. Tomorrow's gonna be a busy day."

Hours later when everyone fell asleep, Logania lay listening to the wind which had softened to an eerie whisper. In the lull she could hear Ardelia coughing laboriously, still sitting in the old rocker by the fire. Logania quietly slipped out of bed and crept down from the loft shivering as her feet touched the cold, damp floor.

"Ma, are you all right?" she whispered, putting her arms around Ardelia.

"Oh, Honey, get back to bed before you catch your death of cold," whispered Ardelia in her husky, cough racked voice.

"No, Ma, I'm fixing you some molasses and tea. That should help you feel better."

Logania bustled about and soon handed a steaming mug of tea to her mother which Ardelia sipped gratefully.

"You know, child that really helped. You always know how to make your old Ma feel better. Now get on to bed. You need your rest," murmured Ardelia.

"Sure, Ma, Logania said, "but I just wanted to ask you—what's this Pennsylvania like? Your Pa and Vinie stayed there a long time. They must have liked it."

"Oh, they did, Honey. They said they liked it just fine. Said it was a beautiful country, lots of farmland and the people easy to get along with. But Pa missed his children back here and I missed him too."

"You know Ma, I think I'd like to visit this Pennsylvania some day," Logania ventured.

"Well, Logania maybe you will child. Maybe you will. Now get on to bed. Tomorrow's gonna be a busy day."

Christmas was only a few weeks away and the Armstead family were all preparing for it. Robert spent all his free time whittling behind the shed. He was working extra hard to finish a stick doll for his little sisters, Bessie and Pearl. For Kelia who was four, he had carved a whistle. The family all looked forward to Christmas. They'd spent the months of October and November dipping candles so they'd have light in the long, dark days ahead. They'd picked and dried apples and berries and stored them in the root cellar under the cabin floor. Whatever the garden yielded at the end of summer was packed away also. Nothing was wasted in the Armstead household.

"Thank the Lord for old Bessie," Ardelia said often. "My young uns always have fresh milk." Pa went hunting every day with Robert and Wash. He hoped to kill a turkey for Christmas dinner. Everyone in the family was excited. Christmas meant a huge meal, something they rarely got. The girls Nannie, Logania, and Mary Lou planned to surprise Ardelia with a new quilt for Christmas. During the year they'd grabbed every scrap of cloth left over from making clothes. They'd even used their old clothes, which had been patched over and over. Now they'd almost completed it, and whenever one of them finished their chores, they'd climb up to the loft to stitch in secret.

A few days before Christmas, Pa caught his turkey and the whole family rejoiced, for that meant a big Christmas dinner and enough meat to last until the New Year. Ardelia and the girls baked bread and pies over the old, temperamental fireplace and Wash was sent to invite Martha and Henry for Christmas dinner.

On Christmas morning everyone rose bright and early. The smell of roasting turkey drifted through the cabin. Ardelia had been up since daybreak preparing food for the big meal. Several pots hung over the fireplace bubbling away. Mary Lou and Logania worked diligently at the kitchen table making the last of the apple pies. Harry and Wash went into the woods to find a few choice stumps to make extra seats. Robert worked diligently to adding a plank to enlarge the kitchen table. Nannie swept the floor. Charles fed the animals. Everyone bustled about doing their best to make this day special. Even little Kay was put in charge of watching his two little sisters to keep them out of trouble.

Outside the day dawned crisp and cold, scattering a dusting of snow on the on the winter hardened ground. Ardelia rejoiced. Good traveling weather. All the guests would be able to come. Ardelia surveyed the cabin. The pies baked in special pots over the fire. Robert finished the table and the girls covered it with a clean white cloth. The cabin was spic and span clean and all the animals fed. Everything was ready.

"All right, you all come eat now," Ardelia called. "Early breakfast today before all our kin come."

Then she surprised everyone with a delicious ripe orange on their plate at the table. "Merry Christmas," she said as they all sat down at the table.

"Ma, thank you for these oranges. They sure make my mouth happy," said Nannie. "Where did you get em, Ma?" asked Robert.

"Now, Robert, stop being so logical and just enjoy my little surprise," answered Ardelia. "What a great day this is going to be," said Mary Lou.

"Let's hurry and finish," whispered Logania. "We have some things to do up in the loft." Then she winked at Nannie.

"Yes, let's hurry," answered Nannie.

After breakfast, the girls all disappeared except for Mary Lou who fed the two youngest. Harry and Wash had returned and now they worked in the yard making the stumps into seats.

Ardelia labored over her cook pots fussing every time a stray spark flew on her well mended dress. Later that afternoon, their guests arrived. Martha with her baby and husband Henry. Pastor Miller from the church, and two of Ardelia's stepbrothers. Harry and Wash added their chairs to the table. Logania set it and soon everyone was seated ready to eat their Christmas dinner.

The little wooden table groaned under its load of food. Pastor Miller stood up to say the blessing as everyone bowed their heads. The blessing droned on and on. Nannie opened one eye and peeked at all that food cooling on the table. When the minister paused to take a breath, Nannie said very loudly, "Amen."

Everyone laughed and the eating began.

Later that evening, Pastor Miller played his fiddle, and all the children danced. The little cabin echoed with music. Then when a waltz was played, Harry grabbed Ardelia's hand and around the cabin they waltzed while the children clapped.

"Now, children," called the Pastor, "I have a Christmas treat for all of you."

"He handed everyone a licorice stick he'd bought at the store in town. The children were thrilled. Seldom did they have sweets. Wash hastily backed away when the minister offered him a treat also.

"Oh no," he muttered. "That's for kids."

Mr. Brown just chuckled and dropped it in his hand.

"Enjoy it anyway, Son," he said. "It's just once a year."

"I have a surprise, too," said Robert. "Kay and Bessie. Look what I made for you. Ma, here's one for little Pearl, too."

"Oh, thank you, Robbie," yelled Kay blowing on his whistle.

"Why, Robert, when did you have time?" Ardelia asked handing the doll to the baby.

"Pretty baby, pretty baby," whispered Bessie. "Thankie Robbie."

"It didn't take long to whittle em and I knew the babies would like em."

"That was very nice of you, Robert," answered Ardelia. "I'm proud of you."

"It wasn't much. I enjoyed making them. Look at Pearl. She's chewing her doll," said Robert smiling.

"It's been a long day," said Ardelia. I think it's time for bed. our kin are staying till tomorrow except Pastor Miller so tell him good night and then off to bed with you."

"Wait, Ma, there's one more thing that wasn't given out yet," called Nannie. Down from the loft came Mary Lou and Logania carrying the quilt "This is for you, Ma," said all of the girls together.

Ardelia picked up the quilt as if it would break. Tears formed in the corners of her eyes.

"Girls, this is beautiful," she whispered. You must have worked so hard on this. It's the best present I ever got."

"It was Logania's idea," piped Nannie. "But we all helped."

Thank you Logania., Nannie, and Mary Lou. I'm gonna treasure this forever." She gave all the children a big kiss on the forehead.

"I truly believe," she said smiling at everyone. "This is one of the best Christmases I ever had."

Everyone crawled into bed that night well fed and tired and thinking it had been a wonderful day.

CHAPTER 2

Pennsylvania

The years passed and Ardelia and her brood struggled on. Wash married a young girl named Betsy and built a house nearby so he could help his Pa on the farm. Harry worked on the old cabin building on additions and Mary Lou had two young ones in quick secession to fill the old house. But the family was dirt poor and winters were extremely hard on the Armstead family. So it was this family Pastor Miller had in mind when he received a letter from Pennsylvania.

A rich family up North wanted a young refined girl to work in their home and care for their infant son. Pastor Miller became acquainted with the Maxwell family when they made a huge donation to several black churches in Albemarle County to support the missionary fund. Pastor Miller, in Pennsylvania on special business for the church, made a special trip to personally thank the Maxwells and became good friends with them When they wanted to employ a young girl, they called Pastor Miller to select a suitable person relying on his good judgment.

Pastor Miller hooked up his buggy and rode out to the Armstead house the very next day. After a very frugal dinner, Pastor Miller gathered the family around the fire.

"Miss Ardelia, I have some good news for you," he said. He glanced at the girls watching him attentively.

"At least I hope you think this is good news," he said clearing his throat. "I know this family in Pennsylvania. They just had a new baby, and they want a young, reliable girl to live in their home and care for the baby.

"They want one of my girls?" asked Ardelia.

"Well, they want someone honest and trustworthy, so naturally I thought of your girls," said the Pastor smiling.

"Why don't they hire someone up there where they live?" asked Harry.

"Their good people," answered the Pastor. "And they want to help a young black girl. They'll pay good wages and she'll have her own room and every Sunday off."

"Who's gonna watch out for my girl way up there?" bellowed Harry.

"Now, Harry," said Pastor Miller the family is a good one. I told you they'll take good care of your daughter."

Ardelia looked at her three older daughters sitting around the fire. Mary Lou was frowning slightly as she fed the baby Ardelia and held little Agnes who kept reaching for the fire. Nannie sat staring at her shoes. Logania watched the Pastor and listened carefully.

"I'll go Ma," said Logania. I've always wanted to see Pennsylvania ever since you told me the stories about your Pa and Vinie. Besides Mary Lou can't go. She has to take care of Agnes and little Delia. And Nannie would be afraid to travel so far from home. But Ma, I would like to do it. I could send you and Pa money to help out and it wouldn't be forever. Would it Pastor Miller?"

"No Logania, of course not. It's on a trial basis. If the Maxwell's feel it's not working out or if you didn't like the job for some reason, they've agreed to pay your fare back home."

Harry slid his chair closer to the fire and patted Logania's long, dark curls.

"You know, Honey, You don't have to do this. We'll manage somehow. We always do. I don't want none of my girls so far away from their family. The Pastor can send some other girl up there," said Harry.

"Oh Logania," whispered Nannie. Your right. I'd be afraid to go, but I don't want you to go either. Whose gonna feed that mean old hen, Sarah? No one can get near her except you, Logania. Besides them Northerners are different then us. Please don't go."

Robert put down his whittling and stood up.

"Pastor Miller, don't they have no jobs up there for men? Girls should stay with their families."

"No, Robert, this was a special request because I know this family. They would take good care of Logania. I didn't think you all would object so much."

Ardelia put her hand on Harry's shoulder.

"Now, Harry," she said. We need the money and besides Logania's always wanted to see Pennsylvania. I don't want none of our girls so far away either, but she can always come back if things don't work out. Pastor Miller would keep in touch and make sure Logania's happy. Wouldn't you, Pastor?"

"I sure will, Ardelia. Look, Harry, this is a respectable family. They can teach Logania things about cooking and etiquette, all kinds of things.

Harry grumbled. "Aint nothing she can learn from them that she can't learn from her own mother."

Logania stood up. "Pa, I really want to go." she said. "Really!"

Harry patted her dark curls again. "It's your choice, Honey," he said. Then he went out the door still grumbling to himself.

"It will be O.K. Pastor," said Ardelia. "I'll talk to him."

"They want her as soon as possible but I guess we could tell two weeks so Logania can get her things together. They've already wired me the train fare," said the Pastor.

"Don't you worry, Pastor. We'll have her ready," said Ardelia. "Thanks for thinking of us."

"Good afternoon, Pastor."

"Good afternoon, Delia."

The next two weeks were busy ones. Mary Lou altered her Sunday frock to fit Logania.

"Can't have you going to Pennsylvania with only one good frock," she said when Logania thanked her.

"Now, Ma, she has to have at least one set of underclothes, and shoes that ain't all worn down, and stockings and of course, a new bonnet."

"Mary Lou, there just ain't no money to buy all that stuff," answered Ardelia. "Oh Ma," moaned Mary Lou. "She don't even have a suitcase."

"Look, Ma," called Robert. "I could put new heels on her shoes and polish them up a bit." "Robbie, that's a good idea. That would be fine. Now for the underclothes."

Ardelia looked around the cabin. Folded neatly under the table was the crisp white tablecloth they used for Christmas dinner.

"This will make a wonderful set of underclothes," she said smiling.

"Oh, Ma," whispered Logania. "Not your tablecloth."

"Nonsense, girl, this will work fine. "Can't have you movin in with them white folks lookin like a beggar."

"She can take my bonnet," piped up Nannie. "I never wear it so it still looks brand new."

"Nannie, I couldn't take your bonnet," said Logania.

"Sure you can," Nannie smiled. "I want to do something to help too. And maybe when you wear it you'll think of me," said Nannie shyly.

Logania sniffed, "That's all I'm going to be doing is thinking of all of you." Charles came forward quietly and dropped a quarter into Ardelia's hand.

"Will that get her stockings, Ma?" he said. "Wash gave me this for helping him clean out the barn. I want Logania to have it."

"Thank you, Charles. This will buy Logania a great pair of stockings. Thank you, child."

"Ma, she still needs a suitcase," persisted Mary Lou.

"Let's get busy, girls and make these undergarments and I'll figure out what to do about that later."

Two days before Logania was to leave, Harry came in one evening carrying a little cardboard suitcase.

"I guess if everybody else can help Logania, I can too," he said. I asked old Master O'Brien. He was glad to help. Said he was right proud of our family, and hopes it works out for Logania."

"That's it, then," said Ardelia. "Our little girl is gonna be just fine."

"Thank you, Pa," whispered Logania. "It will all be O.K. You'll see."

"Logania, child, we sure gonna miss you," he said.

"We sure are, Honey," said Ardelia.

Logania looked around the old cabin. Ardelia's old rocking chair sat by the fire. Nearby sat the pine wood table Pa had built and the stools Robbie had made for Christmas. All the family stood looking at her lovingly.

"I'm sure gonna miss you all," she sighed.

The sky dripped sorrow as the family rode to the train station to see Logania off. Peyton plodded along slowly stumbling every few steps over the mud rutted road. Nannie sat in the corner of the wagon praying with every lurch that the old wagon would break down so Logania would have to stay. Mary Lou sat next to Logania tugging at her bonnet or fussing with her curls every few seconds. Robert and Charles hung off the back trying to catch raindrops on their tongues. Ardelia and Harry sat in the front guiding Peyton through the mist shrouded day. The horizon was a lead gray and the air just sharp enough to make your eyes tear. At least that's what Harry blamed the moisture in his eyes on. Behind them Wash had borrowed a neighbor's wagon, and in that one sat Martha and Betsy and all the young ones.

When they reached the station the train already sat in place belching smoke and grumbling ominously. Just as Ardelia thrust a box filled with food into Logania's hands, the conductor appeared on the platform.

"Come, Honey, I want to help you get settled." called Ardelia. "Harry, bring the suitcase."

"Wait Sissy," Martha called. She hopped down from the wagon to give Logania a big hug.

"Betsy and I want you to have this. We'll give it to you here because we can't take the babies out in the rain." She handed Logania a handkerchief on which they'd embroidered her name.

"You show them Yankees how it's done, Honey," she said as she climbed back in the wagon.

"Thank you, Martha. I'll treasure this forever." called Logania.

Then she headed for the train with the rest of her family following behind. Now standing in front of the huge train with all of her family waving goodbye, young Logania felt her first misgivings. She didn't want to leave her family. What was she doing?

"All Aboard," yelled the conductor.

Harry placed the suitcase on the train, gave her a big kiss and hug, then disappeared to indulge his sadness in private. All the family were yelling their good-byes now and Ardelia was hugging her tightly.

"Don't worry, Honey," she said. "It won't be for long."

I don't want to go Ma, thought Logania but before that thought turned into words, Ardelia handed her an envelope.

"Paster Miller sent it," she said with a smile. "Everyone at the church is so proud of you. They thought you should have this for yourself."

Logania opened the envelope and two crisp one dollar bills fell into her lap. Logania gazed sadly out the small window where she could see all her brothers and sisters watching enviously.

"I'll take good care of her Mam Make sure she gets to Easton safely," the conductor told her Ma.

Pa had returned red eyed to help Ardelia off the train. The whistle blew shrilly.

If you all don't get off you'll be going to Pennsylvania too," the conductor called.

"Good-bye Ma, Pa. I'm gonna miss you all so much," whispered Logania.

"Pastor Miller gonna check on you every week. Don't you worry," yelled Ardelia as Harry guided her back to the platform. "You know God never gives you more than you can bear."

The huge, old locomotive began to move slowly away. Now it gathered speed moving faster and faster. Logania shifted in her seat straining her neck to see out the one small window. There framed in the window stood her whole family still waving, and then the train rounded the bend and they all disappeared from sight.

Logania's eyes burned as she fought to keep the tears back, so it was some time before she noticed the majestic, blue mountains flying by the window. The beautiful Blue Ridge Mountains which surrounded Charlottesville, now whizzing by only emphasized the fact that she was really leaving home. Finally the lump in her throat dissolve slightly and the stinging of her eyes lessened enough for her to peer intently at the rows of wheat growing in the fields. Dozens of little white washed farms sat gleaming in the morning sun. Logania had never been away from home before so every sight was new and wondrous to her untamed eyes.

'Well, little lady, how's it going?" called conductor Sam when he came through to punch the tickets.

"Are you enjoying the trip?"

At Logania's woeful look he smiled. "I know," he said. "You miss your family. But, Honey look at this as an adventure, and I'm sure those people waiting for you up there in Easton are a nice family. It's a nice little town. You'll like it."

"Have you ever been there?" asked Logania.

"Why sure, Honey. I have a cousin that lives there. I visit her often. Now, why don't you unwrap that delicious looking lunch and eat and by the time you eat and have a little nap, we'll be there.

Logania didn't think she would sleep at all but the swaying of the train and the dickety ciack of the wheels soon lulled her to slumber. When she opened her eyes scenery was speeding by the window and Logania realized her stomach was growling incessantly.

Logania carefully unwrapped the box Ardelia had given her. It was tied carefully with a red ribbon, which Logania now untied. the luscious smell of Ardelia's corn meal biscuits covered with honey, floated into the stale cabin air. Also in the box were two small chicken legs and a piece of jelly cake and a small jar of lemonade, now quite warm and sticky. What Ardelia must have sacrificed to include those two small chicken legs. Logania knew how scarce meat had been this winter. Her eyes filled with tears all over again, but she ate every bite of food in the box, enjoying every crumb. She'd just laid the empty box aside when she felt the train slow down and the conductor yell Easton!! Easton, Pennsylvania!!!!!

Logania peered out the window as the train rolled to a—stop. Flakes drifted lazily to the ground from a lead colored sky. The train station sat beside the Delaware River which flowed sluggishly over jagged chunks of ice floating down the river like gigantic ducks.

As old Sam, the conductor helped her off the train, Logania could see a row of horse and carriages lining the street opposite the station. In front of one of the carriages stood a tall black man in a blue hat and coat holding a sign.

"That's you, Honey," Sam said hurrying her along. "That sign he's holding says Miss Logania." He guided-her across the snow covered road and up to the carriage.

"This here's Miss Logania," he told the man with the sign. Then he patted her bonnet.

"You Lake care; Honey," he said and then he handed the tall, black man—her suitcase and hurried back to the train. Another blast echoed across the station and then the train chugged away off to the next destination.

The tall man tipped his hat. "Well," he said. "Miss Logania, We better get moving. The Maxwells are anxious to meet you. Just climb into the carriage and we'll be going."

Soon as Logania was tucked into the seat the driver took off through the city. The old carriage jerked from side to side on the ice rutted road. Logania struggled vainly to keep her bonnet on straight and then finally yanked it off in frustration.

"Are you a soldier?" she called grabbing onto the seat to keep from falling.

The driver chuckled, "Am I going too fast for you? No, Miss Logania, I'm not a soldier. I'm just the driver, Joseph. I drive the Maxwells anywhere they want to go."

Logania looked out the window. There seemed to be carriages everywhere, and down the middle of the street trolley cars shrieked their brakes and headed straight for her.

"Where are they all going? she gasped as a horse trotted by so close, she could feel his hot breath.

"Well, Miss Logania, you in the city now, but you'll soon get used to this. Now see up there ahead. Up that hill, you see all those trees?"

"Sure, I can see em," she panted trying to shove her suitcase back under the seat. "That's where we're going. That's College Hill. That building up ahead is Lafayette College where the young, white gentlemen go. Mrs. Maxwell lives just a little bit yonder." Minutes later, Joseph slowed down. Logania looked up and gasped. In front of her was the biggest house she'd ever seen. Ardelia wouldn't have believed it. Four of their little cabins could fit into it. Several acres away sat another huge building which Joseph called a stable.

"Come on, Miss Logania, called Joseph. "I see Miss Sally is waiting at the door for us." Logania started up the path when a little white ball of fluff launched itself at her.

"Come on, Honey," called Miss Sally. "That's just Snowball, Mrs. Maxwell's cat. She greets everybody."

Logania had felt so lonely and sad, but now she sat on the ground giggling softly as the enormous white cat licked her face. Finally Joseph persuaded her to leave the cat and proceed into the house. The main hallway stunned her into silence again. It was huge and everywhere she looked sat beautiful pieces of art. Then she was led through a room where the only furniture was a gleaming walnut table surrounded by chairs and an enormous chest loaded with gorgeous china.

Miss Sally caught her staring and said, "This here's the dining room. Mr. and Mrs. Maxwell are waiting for you in the library."

Logania looked up. "What's a library?" she asked.

"Lord, Honey, you'11 get used to it. That's where they keep shelves and shelves of books. Now you'll see everything later. The Maxwells are waiting to see you."

As they entered the library, the first thing Logania noticed was the vast fireplace and nearby a distinguished looking man smoking a pipe. Across from him sat the most attractive woman she'd ever seen. She had raven black hair and blue eyes like a clear summer sky. As Logania approached, she stood and came forward.

"You must be Miss Armstead. Welcome to our home. How was your trip?" she asked.

"It was just fine," responded Logania.

"Really? Just fine? Even the part when our Joe picked you up'

"Well," Logania said, smoothing her battered bonnet.

"I thought so", she said and gave a tinkling little laugh. "Our Joe always thinks he's on the race track."

"How old is she?" came a deep voice from the corner. "She doesn't look old enough to care for no one, let alone our son. How old are you, Miss?"

Logania straightened her shoulders. "It's Miss Armstead, sir and I'm nineteen, near twenty and I been caring for my brothers and sisters for years."

"Pardon me for saying so, Miss Armstead, but you don't look wet behind the ears to me."

"Henry!! Don't frighten the child. Pastor Miller recommended her. You just leave her get settled before you start in," said Mrs. Maxwell. "Come on Logania, I'll show you the baby and then you can rest in your room awhile till dinner. Miss Sally is putting your clothes away now."

Alice Maxwell hurried to the doorway, but Logania stopped and looked back.

"Mr. Maxwell," she said. I nursed my Ma and my Pa, all of my brothers and sisters, I've chopped wood, worked in the fields, slaughtered chickens, helped birth a foal, rode a horse and I'm sure I can take care of one little baby."

Down long hallways they walked which seemed to go on forever, then up a grand stair case, so polished, she could see her reflection, and then down more hallways lined with dozens of pictures, and then finally Alice Maxwell stopped.

"This is the nursery" she said.

Then she opened the door. The room was painted a pale blue. In one corner sat a huge old rocking chair. In the other a carved rocking horse for the baby. Beautiful old chests lined the walls and on one side sat an antique crib gleaming in the pale afternoon light.

Lying in it fast asleep, a dark hair angel slept. Only about a month old, he lay on his tummy sucking one tiny thumb, his little behind stuck up in the air.

"He's gorgeous," Logania whispered. "What's his name?"

"Henry Andrew III, but we call him Hank," responded Alice. "Such a little guy for such a big name. Come on now, your room is right next door so you can hear him at night. This is your room," she said opening the door.

The walls were covered with roses and in one corner sat a huge brass bed and the closet looked enormous with Logania's few belongings in it. Logania walked the length of the room slowly. She couldn't get over the size of the room.

"Now, I'm going to let you rest a bit. Miss Sally will bring you some water up so you can tidy up a bit before dinner. We'll talk after you've rested. I'm sure everything is going to work out just fine." Then she left, her petticoats rustling down the hall and the smell of some sweet sachet she wore, gradually fading.

Logania still missed her family but she slipped into her new life like an old glove. Henry Jr. flourished under her tender care, and Henry Sr. never again voiced an objection, as he watched his son blossom under her touch.

One Sunday afternoon several months after she arrived, Logania sat in the fabulous gardens outside the stable talking to the horses. Sable, with her big brown eyes was her favorite. Mrs. Maxwell stood watching her from the window. When Logania returned to the house, she called her.

"Logania," she said. "You know Sunday is your day off and you may do anything you want. A young girl like you must want to go shopping sometime or maybe go to church. Didn't Pastor Miller tell me you loved to go to church?"

"I do love to go to church," answered Logania, but I'm a stranger here and I'd be afraid to go alone."

"Now, Logania, I hear there's a colored church downtown. Miss Sally use to go. She doesn't go much anymore, but I'm sure Joe would take you if you'd like to go." It would be a great place to meet other young people your age. Would you want to go next Sunday?"

"That's a wonderful idea, Mrs. Maxwell. I sure would. I'm gonna ask Miss Sally all about it right now."

In the kitchen Sally was baking pies, but she loved to talk to Logania. Logania perched on one of the chairs and nibbled on an apple.

"Miss Sally?" she asked. "Did you ever go to the colored church downtown?"

"Lord, yes, Honey. It's a real nice church called the AME or something like that. Don't go much anymore though. My legs just get too stiff sitting so long, but you would enjoy it Honey. Are you planning on going?"

"If Joe will take me next Sunday," sighed Logania.

"Oh, I know old Joe will be glad to take you, but Logania, Honey?"

"Yes, Miss Sally."

"Don't you think you could use some of your wages to get some new shoes and maybe a new Sunday frock."

"That's the very next thing I was fixing to ask you," said Logania. 'Would you take me shopping?"

"Sure, Honey, there's nothing I like better than spending money even if it's not my own. I hear they have a sale at Farr Brothers and Co. That's the shoe store. I say about five dollars will buy a whole outfit including a ribbon to tie up that pretty hair."

Logania had been sending money every two weeks to her family via Pastor Miller, but she had quite a bit put aside for herself since she hadn't spent anything since moving to Easton. So Miss Sally and Logania went shopping. Logania found the perfect new boots for two dollars, a new dress for two dollars, and she even had a dollar left to buy a pretty white ribbon for her hair and a sandwich for her and Miss Sally in the only restaurant on Northampton Street. It was the first time Logania had been downtown and she walked poor Miss Sally all around the circle taking in all the sights. Finally they went to the corner where Joe had left them off, and there he was waiting with the carriage to take them home. All the way home Logania chattered gaily. Miss Sally smiled over her head at Joe.

"Nothing like shopping to make a young girl happy," she whispered to Joe as Logania talked on.

CHAPTER 3

Levi

The next Sunday, Joe got out the old carriage and drove Logania to church. When they reached the church Pastor Samuel stood in the doorway greeting the congregation. As Logania approached, he stepped forward. "Welcome to the AME Church Miss,Miss

"This is Miss Armstead, Pastor," said Joe. "She's new in town. She's working for the Maxwell's."

"Welcome Miss Armstead. I'm sure you'll enjoy our services today."

"I'm sure I will," responded Logania shyly.

Joe led her to a pew near the back of the church and then turned to leave.

"Joe, you mean you're not going to stay. Your gonna leave me here all alone."

"You'll be fine, Honey" answered Joe. "Now just relax and enjoy the service. I'll be waiting for you where the carriage is now when it's over."

Logania sat down nervously, but soon the familiar music and responses put her at ease and she found herself enjoying the service enormously. Things went fine until after Pastor Samuel gave his sermon and the offering was collected, then he stepped up to the pulpit and said, "before we sing our last hymn today, I would like to introduce two visitors who we hope will join our congregation. Please stand up when I call your name. We have Miss Armstead and Mr. Jackson, our two newcomers today."

Logania timidly stood up as a young man down in front got up slowly too. There were murmurs from the congregation of "welcome sister, welcome brother, the Lord welcomes you, and God Bless You." As Logania glanced around, she saw only a blur of smiling faces until she caught a glimpse of a distinguished looking gentlemen two rows behind her, and he was staring straight at her.

He had piercing brown eyes, long aristocratic nose over a neatly trimmed mustache and dark, wavy hair just brushing his collar, and what a collar. It stood up stiffly starched and crisply white. A black tie over a matching vest and jacket completed the ensemble. All this Logania noticed in the seconds before she reclaimed her seat. A little flustered, she fanned her face with the hymn book. What a magnificent looking man, she thought.

Behind her the man, Levi was whispering urgently to his friend, Will, "Who is she? She's the prettiest young woman I've ever seen. I've got to meet her."

"Look, Levi, I don't know her but after church, just find out from her driver where she lives and you can write her a letter or something."

"Will, you know I can't read or write. What am I going to do?"

"Levi, will you shush," Will whispered. "Everyone is staring at us. Just have the driver introduce you. Maybe she'll be interested."

After the service Levi did get himself introduced to Logania, but she simply looked at him with those cool, dark eyes and said "I'm pleased to meet you but I must be going now." Then she climbed quickly into the carriage and adjusted her bonnet never meeting his eyes again. Levi stood watching the carriage until it disappeared from sight feeling completely deflated. Then he turned to his friend who was just exiting the church.

"Will, you're going to write that letter for me tonight," he said. "I've never met anyone like her before. I'm going to marry her."

A few days after Logania's visit to church, a letter arrived from Charlottesville marked urgent, addressed to her. Logania hurried to the kitchen where Sally was preparing dinner.

"Miss Sally, Miss Sally, please read this to me," pleaded Logania. "Has something Happened?"

"Dear Miss Logania," Sally read I'm sorry I have very sad news for you. Your mother passed away last night. It was very sudden, but you know how often she had bouts of illness as you use to care for her so often. She was very proud of you. All of your brothers and sisters want you to remain there. They are very sad, but they appreciate all the help you've sent and they don't want you making that dangerous trip alone again. There is really nothing you can do anyway. Even your father, Harry would prefer that you stay.

Take care Logania,
Sincerely,
Pastor Lee Miller

"No! oh no! It can't be true. I can't face this. I can't I can't," Logania cried as tears streamed down her cheeks.

"Oh Honey," whispered Sally. "I'm sorry. She held Logania tightly while she wept in her arms.

Finally when some of the pain lessened, Logania whispered, "I have to go home."

"Logania, sweetheart, now listen to me," said Sally. "Your folks is right. What can you do now? Besides they don't want you to make that trip alone again. They will all understand. Remember your Ma like she was.

"I should never have left," weeped Logania. I should have stayed in Charlottsville. I wouldn't let her die. I wouldn't."

"Honey, you know that ain't true. You can't change the Lord's way. Maybe your poor Ma was just worn out. Plain tired of being sick. Maybe she wanted to go home."

"I won't ever see my Ma, again," sobbed Logania. "I won't ever see her."

"Honey, I know you believe in God and if you believe, I'm sure you know you'll see your Ma again someday. Now, Honey, I'm gonna tell Alice what happened, and then I'm gonna take you up to your room and try to get you to calm down and relax."

Hours later as darkness fell, Logania lay alone, her mind forming the same question over and over. Why God? Why my Ma?

When Sally brought a platter of food to her room, she waved her away tiredly. Her throat felt swollen shut, all clogged up with grief as it was.

"Look, Honey," said Sally. "Alice wanted to come in but I thought you'd rather be alone right now. She and Henry are sending money to your Pa to use as he sees fit. They really want you to stay on, but it's your choice."

Logania peered at her out of her swollen, reddened eyes.

"I'm staying," she whispered tiredly. "Your right. There's nothing I can do, now, but I don't think I'll ever get over this."

The next day when Logania awoke, she was astonished to see the sun shining brightly, birds twittering as usual, and baby Henry crying for his breakfast. The world continued on as if nothing had happened, though Logania felt as though her world had ended. One month after her mother's death, Logania received another letter. She stared at the unfamiliar writing for a long time before taking it to Sally.

"I think it's from that man I met at the church," she said pulling the letter from the envelope and handing it to Sally.

"Would you read it please?" she asked.

Sally gazed at the letter for a few seconds and then said, "I don't think I should. It's a love letter meant for you only."

"Please read it, Sally. If it waits till I can read it, I'll be an old woman." Sally; read: My dearest Logania, I fear you misunderstood my intentions on Sunday, at the church. Maybe you thought it rude that I imposed myself upon you in that way. What you don't understand, my dear, is that the minute I saw you I fell in love. You may think this impossible, but it can happen as I am the perfect example. My greatest desire is that one day you will be my wife. You probably think me crazy as we know nothing about each other and have never been alone together, but I knew when I saw you, it was the real thing. I hope next Sunday you will let me escort you to church so you will get to know me better, but in my heart, Logania you are already part of my future.

—

With deepest respect for you,
Levi

Sally fanned herself briskly with the letter. "My goodness, Logania. That young man is smitten with you. Whatever did you do to him?"

Logania smiled a little smile which didn't quite erase the sadness in her eyes.

"I just looked at him. I did think he was rather handsome, but he's a total stranger. He couldn't possibly love me from one look. Maybe he is a little crazy."

"What are you going to do, Honey? Are you going to go to church with him? asked Sally.

"Oh, yes, I do owe him a reply. Don't I? I see no harm in going to church with him, but as for even thinking about marriage, that's quite impossible."

"O.K., Sweetie, I'll write a short note back to him telling him you'll go to church and then it will be up to you."

Bright and early Sunday morning Levi was there with his horse and buggy. After they left, Sally fussed all day about the two of them going off alone together. Much later that day when Logania returned, she told Sally "I'm twenty years old. I'm no baby anymore. Since my mother died, I've grown up. All I could think of before was getting this job over, so I could go home to Ma."

Sally answered, "Logania, Honey, there ain't nothing wrong in wanting to be near your Ma." Logania took a bite of the sandwich Sally handed her.

"You know, Sally," she said. My sister Martha has nine children, now. Nine Mary Lou has two daughters. Even Wash, who told me he was never getting married, has a son. I'm just saying I guess it's time for me to start thinking along those lines too."

Sally smiled. "Could this new thinking have anything to do with the fact that Mr. Levi brought you back two hours after church was over today?"

"He is a very interesting person to talk to. He took me riding by the river and we talked about just everything. He told me he's working on building the new Easton High School. Imagine being able to tell your children one day, you helped build the school they're going to.

"Honey, it sounds like you were pretty impressed by him," said Sally.

"I do enjoy talking to him but I'm not quite ready for anything more yet."

During the weeks that followed Logania and Levi had more and more outings together. They enjoyed time together, but Levi who was older than Logania was interested in marriage and he was doing all he could to turn Logania's thoughts in that direction also.

One evening Levi and Logania were returning from a church supper. It was early September and Levi suggested they stop in the woods and see the fall colors. Logania agreed. The air smelled of pine trees and the tangy smell of ripe berries. As they moved into the forest Logania looked up. Overhead was a rainbow of color, golden yellow, burnt orange, fire red. Above them stretched a golden arch for miles.

Logania sighed. "You can't say we aren't rich," she said, "Look at all that gold up there God has given us."

Levi spread out the old blanket he'd brought from the wagon on the ground. "Here, Honey, lie down and enjoy the sight."

Logania stretched out on the blanket and so did Levi. In the returning quiet, the forest sounds began again. Bees buzzing briskly from flower to flower, squirrels scurrying through the dry leaves looking for nuts, birds of every type, some chirping daintily, others cawing, loud and raucous in their search for food. Logania lay watching the fading sunlight turn the leaves to shades of copper and brown, and Levi lay watching the intriguing expressions going across her face.

"You, know, Honey, you are beautiful," he said.

Logania smiled. "I'm not really," she said, "but I'm glad you think so."

Levi bent down and kissed her lightly, and was quite startled when she returned the kiss. He pulled her closer and Logania felt a little flurry of excitement pass through her and then it kept growing and growing. This was what her sisters had whispered and giggled about during the night when they were supposed to be sleeping. This feeling of excitement and need. She wanted Levi closer. Suddenly he was lowering his pants and she was helping him. She didn't want this feeling to end. She helped him lift her skirts. All the forest noises faded out as Levi and Logania joined together on the blanket. Wave after wave of feeling shuddered through her body and then slowly she returned to planet Earth. Levi was shame faced and rapidly pulling up his trousers.

"I'm sorry, Honey, I didn't mean for it to go that far. I really didn't. You just looked so pretty lying there."

Logania calmly adjusted her skirts. Levi awkwardly folded up the blanket still turned away from her. Logania took his face in her hands and turned him toward her.

Taking his hand gently in hers, Logania said, "Levi, Honey, it's time we planned our wedding."

All the way back home in the carriage, Levi couldn't stop smiling. "I've already picked out our house, Honey, and you can keep working if you want, but you don't have to. Will will be my best man but—

"Lord, Levi," Logania interrupted, "You sure are excited. Everything is going to work out just fine."

The weeks following were very busy as Logania prepared for her wedding. Sally was ecstatic Her Logania was getting married. Sally, right away enlisted one of her sewing friends to make Logania's wedding gown. Now she had to get the material.

"Sally, I'll just wear one of my Sunday frocks. I just cannot afford a wedding dress. Levi wants to get married right away and I think we should, too," pleaded Logania.

Two days later, Mrs. Maxwell had Sally clean out the attic. She'd almost finished when she discovered a huge carton box tied and stacked in the corner. On the top someone had written DO NOT TOUCH, so naturally Sally touched it. She opened it and yards and yards of glorious white material fell out soft and in perfect condition, and then the mask fell out. It was a Ku Klux Klan outfit in Mrs. Maxwell's attic. She couldn't believe it. When she showed it to Alice, she couldn't believe it either.

"No one in our family has ever even thought of being in something so vulgar," she said angrily. "It must have been up there when we bought the house. That's why I asked you to clean the attic. We're throwing away all that junk stored up there that doesn't belong to us. We are going to build a playroom up there for Henry when he gets older."

Sally said thoughtfully, "Then you don't want this uniform?"

"Are you kidding? Alice shivered. "Get it out of my sight. It's ghastly!! Destroy it!! Do whatever you want with it."

Sally showed it to Logania. "It makes me angry to even look at it," she said.

Sally smiled. "In this form, Yes. But, now picture this beautiful soft white material in a glorious floor length gown, trimmed in white satin and lace."

Logania stared at her. "You mean a wedding gown.!"

"Of course. The material is perfect for it and what a laugh on the person that used this to make his weapon of terror into a symbol of love."

Logania laughed. She chuckled till the tears ran down her face. "Sally, you really are something and your right. We can't ever tell anyone though. It will be our secret:'

The seamstress never saw the mask, only the yards of white material and she made a beautiful gown. Logania's sisters sent her lace and their apologies because they couldn't be there, and Sally contributed the satin. The gown, when finished was stunning. The high neck was trimmed in lace as were the sleeves. A white satin bow around the waist with just a slight bustle. Logania bought a little white hat which perched on the beautiful bun that Sally wound her long hair into. So on October 01, 1901, Logania became Mrs. Logania Mills and no one ever knew the secret of her wedding gown, but Logania laughed about it often.

The wedding was beautiful. They married in the AME church with just a few close friends present. The minister Paster Rankin was a friend of Levi's, so he performed the ceremony. Afterwards Mrs. Maxwell allowed Logania and her friends to hold a small gathering on her patio at which Sally served a menu of fried chicken, potato salad, collard greens, and wedding cake with fresh cold lemonade. Levi was anxious to get his new bride home, so the party ended early. Mrs. Maxwell told Logania to have a great weekend off and Sally hugged and kissed her.

"God Bless You, Logania," she said, and don't forget to come back next week." Then Levi helped his new bride into the carriage and off they rode to their new home.

CHAPTER 4

Their First Home

Levi and Logania were on the road to their new home. In record time they approached the little house on Snyder Street. It was a small house, only two rooms downstairs, but three bedrooms. a small outhouse was built close by, but to Logania her own home at last, it seemed like a palace. Levi insisted on carrying Logania over the threshold and then set her down on the one lone chair in the living room. Logania peeked in the kitchen. Besides the huge coal stove and small ice box in the corner, Levi had built and polished to perfection a complete dinette set. Logania ran her hand across it lovingly.

"It's beautiful, Honey," she whispered. "How hard you must have worked on this."

"With the bedroom furniture, it's all I can afford right now, but we'll get everything we need real soon, Honey."

"Lee, it's just wonderful to have our own home. We'll get everything we need in good time. Remember, patience is a virtue."

"O.K. Honey, I'm going to get some wood and build a fire. It's going to get pretty cold tonight. Now you just put something on comfortable and I'll have both these stoves going in no time."

It felt strange to Logania packing away her clothes in the great armoire next to Levi's. Carefully she packed away the wedding dress still chuckling about it's origin. Lastly she unpacked the boxes from Sally and Mrs. Maxwell.

In Sally's box was an exquisite crocheted bedspread, the perfect gift for a new bride and a complete set of dishes for four. In Mrs. Maxwell's box was a matching tablecloth and two silver candle holders. Logania's eyes filled with tears. She was remembering the crisp, white tablecloth her own mother had cut up so she could go up North with fresh new underwear.

Slipping on a pretty blue dress, Logania investigated the rest of the house. She could tell Levi had tried to clean it up for her, but it wasn't quite up to her standards. She'd take care of that tomorrow. Right now she was going to prepare the first meal in her new home.

First she spread the beautiful tablecloth on the shining table. Levi was still outside chopping wood. She could hear him. He was humming Rock Of Ages.

Then she set the table with the new dishes Sally gave her. After some searching, Logania discovered two fat white candles in a kitchen closet which she put in the two silver candle holders. Then she unpacked one more box Sally had given her. It was all the leftover food. God Bless Sally, thought Logania. She wouldn't have to cook tonight. Plenty of chicken, potato salad, and greens left over. Levi had the old stove going by now, so they could even have a hot cup of tea.

By the time Levi had the stove in the living room going, Logania had the table set, the food out, and Levi and Logania sat down and had their first meal together in their own house. Afterwards Levi heated water to wash the dishes while Logania went to change her clothes. She felt a little nauseous and she suspected their tryst in the woods that September day was about to bear fruit. She hadn't yet told Levi but she would tonight.

Later on that evening snuggled together in the big old bed, Logania told Levi there was going to another little Mills.

"That's wonderful, Honey," he whispered. "Another little you for me to love. It's perfect. You've made me so happy."

"Lee, Honey, it won't be easy. It means more money to spend and I'll have to quit work eventually."

"Don't you worry, my love. I'll take care of everything."

"Things don't always work so easily, love. President McKinley alive one minute, dead the next. That's how life really is. Unknowns around every corner."

"We won't let things like that happen to us." Levi hugged her tight. "I'll make sure of it."

Logania smiled. "Oh, Lee, you can't control life. Only God can do that."

"I'm sure gonna try then. This little one that's coming is going to have the best life I can provide."

Logania said nothing. She'd grown up watching her mother stretch every penny till it screamed. She knew what babies meant to the budget. But she just hugged her Levi and they fell asleep.

Five months later on February tenth, little Bertha was born. She was a beautiful child. Curly brown hair and big brown eyes, soft tawny colored skin and a loving smile.

Logania had only a mid wife to help her, but she'd seen her mother have enough babies to know what to expect. After twelve hours of labor, she was exhausted but happy. Back home in Charlottesville, when her sisters would giggle and talk up in the loft. Her younger sister Bessie would say, "when I have my first child, I'm gonna name her Bertha. I love that name. I hate my name Bessie, and your name Logania.""Whoever heard of a Logania?"

So Logania named her first born Bertha and years later when her sister Bessie had her first and named her Bertha too, they had a good laugh about it.

Logania had always thought her name a little odd too, so she named all of her children as different from the name of Logania as she could get. Three years later little Bertella was born. Logania combined the names of Bertha and Ella which would be the name of her next child, Ella. Little Bertella never quite forgave her for that particular name though.

By then Logania could no longer work with three little ones to take care of.so every week became a struggle to survive. One day Logania went to the Second Hand Shop on 4th and Pine spent seven dollars on an old pram which she could load all three little ones in. Then every day she'd take them for walks. Down to Riverside Park to feed the pigeons and watch the Delaware River. Sometimes she'd take them to parades or out when a public figure would come to town. Logania would take her little brood to anything she felt would interest them.

At home she planted a small garden and though they were poor, no one ever went hungry in Logania's house. Despite the three little ones which took a lot of attention, Logania's home always looked spotless. White starched curtains at the windows, the linoleum, no matter how worn, always sparkled newly waxed, and no baby ever dared lay it's head down without a clean, crisp, white sheet under it. Whenever the family was forced to move because they could no longer afford the rent, Logania would swallow her pride and help Levi move into another house.

Little Bertha had just turned six so she was all excited about starting school.

CHAPTER 5

Bertha

Bertha was going to school. She couldn't contain her excitement. For the past year she'd sit little Ella in the old pram and made little Bertella, she called her Bert, sit on a rock next to the pram and they played school. Bertha would be the teacher tapping angrily on the ground when they didn't pay attention. Now, she herself, was going to school.

Logania struggled to get Bertha new clothes for school, but in the end, everything came from a second hand store, it being all that she could afford. The shoes little Bertha wore were two sizes too big, but her clothes though worn, were starched and ironed to perfection.

Bertha proudly carried her pencils and tablet, even though it was packed in a shoe box and tied with a string. Logania walked her to school, her two babies Ella and Bertella still in the pram. Sadly she watched Bertha walk in the door in her boat sized shoes and worn clothes surrounded by all the rich, white children with their shiny new pencil boxes and their brand new clothes. Logania parked the old pram by the door and lifted baby Ella. Little Bertella trotted alongside holding her hand, while Bertha walked in front. School, she was finally going to school and she was ecstatic.

A trim, young woman in a blue suit detached herself from behind a desk and came forward. "Can I help you, Mam?" she addressed Logania.

"We're looking for the kindergarten room. "My little one is supposed to start school today." The woman surveyed Bertha ruefully from her curly braids to the too large shoes on her feet. "Are you sure you have the right school—Miss—Mrs.—?

"Mrs. Mills," stated Logania. "And yes, I'm sure we have the right school. McCartney School!! Just check your list for Bertha Mills. I enrolled her months ago."

Miss Wood, sashayed back to her desk and after flipping through a few papers, she looked up.

"Your right," she said. "Her room is room 102 just down the hall."

"Much obliged," Logania said to Miss Wood, who was still flipping through papers as if she couldn't believe her own eyes. She hoisted Ella to her shoulders and grabbed Bertella's hand and together they walked young Bertha to her room.

She bent down at the doorway and gave her a big kiss.

"I'll be back at 12:00 to take you home. Now you have a good day at school."

"Sure Mommy," Bertha said with a smile. "I'll be fine."

Then proudly she walked into the room and took a seat right in the front.

The teacher wrote on the blackboard Rachel Johnson.

"I'm Miss Johnson," she told the class when everyone was seated, "but you can call me Miss Rachel because I'm going to call all of you by your first names and I think we can get to know each other better that way. Now, I have to make sure everyone is here, so I'm going to call your name and you must answer present, understand?'

As the teacher called the names, Bertha looked around. Everything was so shiny and new. Across the top of the blackboard sat the alphabet in big blue letters, the large letters and the small. She knew cause she had practiced them all summer on a piece of slate from someone's roof and a rock she'd found that wrote white. Across the other board ran a little train and in every car was written a number up to ten. She knew her numbers too.

"Bertha Mills," called the teacher.

I'm present," said Bertha smiling and Miss Rachel smiled back.

"Robert Franklin." On she went with the roll call as Bertha became aware of two little girls behind her giggling. They were pointing at her shoes and whispering back and forth. Bertha looked around again. Every child she looked at was dressed in new clothes and had shiny new shoes that fit. Also as far as she could see, she was the only little girl with brown skin. Then she turned around and looked directly at the two girls who were whispering and giggling.

"What are you laughing at?" she said to the one with blue eyes and blonde hair. "I don't see nothing funny."

"Your shoes," giggled her red hair friend. "There too big, and is that your pencil box? It's just an old shoe box."

"Besides," said the blonde. "Your skin looks dirty. Nobody else looks like that."

"What's your name?" growled Bertha.

"My name is Tammy Lee Watson," said the little girl. "Why do you want to know?"

"Well, my name is Bertha Mills and my skin is dark because I'm a different race from you, and just because I don't have shiny new things like you don't make you no better than me. My Mommy tells me every day I was made by God and God Don't Make No Junk!"

Tammy stopped laughing and shut up. Her little friend turned around too. Bertha turned around to face the teacher smiling. Now she was ready to learn.

And learn she did. Miss Rachel was surprised at the ease with which Bertha learned and also with the way she handled herself in an all white class. She was feisty and smart and soon had the whole class respecting her.

Logania was very proud of her daughter and marveled at the papers she brought home with gold stars on. In the little house on Snyder Street, there wasn't much room, but she gave Bertha her own drawer to keep all her special school stuff in.

The family was very poor, but Logania could always find something to laugh about. In winter they'd gather around the old stove and Bertha would tell what they'd did in school that day. Bertella would listen wide eyed and even baby Ella would coo and babble.

Levi was proud of his family too, but in the days when he was wooing Logania, he hadn't expected so many little ones to be responsible for, the continual chores of supplying food and clothing, worrying about sick children, so when things got too rough, he up and leave for High Springs, Florida where his family lived, leaving Logania to manage alone. And manage she did, and always with a smile. (I never met a kinder or gentler person than my grandmother and I don't think, I ever will).

At Christmas there was special food and at least one brand new store bought present for each of the children. They received at least two baskets of food a year usually around Christmas time, and some second hand toys which Logania accepted gratefully. In 1910 Logania had her first little boy whom she named Richard. Young Bertha was doing brilliantly in school and now young Bertella was anxious to start as the daily sessions of playing school with sister Bertha had her all enthused about school too.

CHAPTER 6

Bertella

When Bertella started McCartney School, Bertha had been going for three years. She was very smart in school and all the teachers liked her. This little black girl with so much spunk amazed them.

Then Bertella started school. From the first it was different. When the other children made fun of her worn clothes, she'd sit in her seat depressed and miserable until the bell rang. Bertha, who had a slew of friends by now, would say, "Bert, stick up for yourself. There only kids. You show them your just as good as they are. And if they still tease you, well who needs em anyway."

But Bertella would Sit in misery until time to go home. The teachers thought maybe she was slow, for she rarely spoke until one day, Miss Johnson found her alone in the music room playing the piano. She stayed in the background until Bertella finished playing, then she came forward.

"Why, that was beautiful, Bert. Where did you learn to play?""I didn't," stuttered Bertella. "I don't know how to play.""But you just played that lovely song. You must've had lessons.""No," said Bertella., "I just saw the piano and started to play." Miss Johnson came forward and gave her a hug.

"Looks like you've been keeping your light under a barrel, Bert. You have a great talent. Now in class, why don't you ever answer or finish your work?"

"The other kids make fun of me," whispered Bertella.

"Well," said Miss Johnson, "I'll put a stop to that and we'll see how you do then." Under Miss Johnson's protection, Bertella bloomed. She was soon at the top of her class and Miss Johnson let her play the piano in the music room when all the other children had recess. After talking to Miss Johnson, little Bert regained her confidence. The next year, she begged from Mrs. Maxwell, apiece of material. Then she talked a neighbor into giving her their old newspapers. From Mommy, she got a needle and thread. Then for two weeks with a newspaper picture to guide her, she created a dress for herself. Each of the children had chores to do, but every day Bertella worked on her dress till she got it perfect.

So the year Bertella went to second grade, she started school in a brand new dress and Mommy rewarded her with a pair of brand new stockings. She started school that year with a whole new attitude.

Miss Johnson was amazed at the Mills children. She'd never considered herself prejudiced. But these two black children from the same family were more talented than half the class.

> Now when Logania walked them to school, it was Richard who lay in the old pram and Ella walked along side. She wasn't as anxious to go to school as her sister because she wanted to stay home with Mommy and help her. Besides she got sick a lot. Colds seemed to stay with her the entire winter. She'd rather stay home and take care of her baby brother Richard though she was rarely more than a baby herself.

When Ella and Richard started school within two years of each other, things were getting really tight. Logania tried again to work for awhile to keep all her children in school and in clothes. She struggled on and when friends said to her how do you manage? All those children and Levi taking off anytime he wants.

Logania would smile that famous gentle smile and say, "God never puts on us anymore then we can bear."

In 1915 Logania had to stop working because she was pregnant again. Having babies so close together was draining and she'd worked hard all her life. When little Theodore was born, Logania made up her mind there would be no more babies. But her plan was doomed for failure for the very next year Robert (we all called him Bobby) was born.

Bobby was different than the rest, where all the Mills children were doing well in school, winning honors many, Bobby seemed uninterested. He daydreamed a lot. Talked gibberish, the teachers said. Some even whispered the word retarded. But we will find out later, all is not always as it seems.

Not long after Bobby was born, Logania became pregnant again. She was in despair. She loved all her children, but she wanted no more as she couldn't depend on Levi, and everyday was a struggle to survive. Perhaps her state of mind and stress affected the child as well, for little Florence was still born. Logania grieved for her lost daughter, and Levi was also very distressed. He felt he deserved a great deal of the blame for this disaster, though lately he'd suffered bouts of sickness which kept him confined to bed. Logania couldn't afford to grieve for long though, as she had six other lives in her hands to keep on the right track. When the rest of the household slept, in those silent still moments just before dawn, Logania would pray for her lost angel. The other children were doing marvelously in school, except for Bobby who daydreamed a lot in class, but Logania knew that Bobby was special. Mothers know.

Years later, when Logania thought her child bearing years over, Rebecca was born easing some of the pain of the loss of Florence. From the start she was a delightful baby, never cried, always healthy, always with a ready smile. The other children all loved to baby sit their sister Rebecca. Logania though worried. After Rebecca's birth Levi seemed exceptionally tired and weak, though he tried to work. His children talented as they were, were being forced to quit school one by one to support the household. First young Bertha, then Bertella, who cried for two weeks afterwards, and then young Teddy who excelled in sports. Still the whole family was shocked when Levi died suddenly of Malaria Fever at his family home in Florida. No hope of anyone returning to school. Logania taught her children that God knows best, but sometimes even she wondered. She remembered how Bert had worked so hard in school until she was at the top of her class. She'd written beautiful poetry and could recite it by ear. Many a day she'd run all the way home from school.

"Mommy, Mommy, I got an award," she'd say soon as she opened the door.

Then Logania grab her and hug her and say "I'm so proud of you, Honey. "I'll hang it right up where everyone can see it. All my children are so smart. My Ardelia was right."

"Who is Ardelia, Mommy?" Bertella would ask.

"That was my Mom, Honey, and she use to be a slave. She always told us that we'd have a better life than her and to learn all you could in this world. And she was right. I can barely write my name, but all my children can read and write and now their bringing home awards. God has truly blessed this household."

Bertella peered puzzled at her mother. "But, Mommy we're so poor. Bertha, Ella, and even Richard and Teddy. We all have to wear hand me downs to school and carry our lunches in shoe boxes. Do you call that a blessing?"

Sweet baby, I know, but we've always had a home to live in, plenty of food to eat and we have the love of each other. That's important. Remember that, Honey. No matter what happens in life, you always have your family to lean on and that's how it should be."

Now Logania spent long, lonely nights weeping into her pillow. It wasn't fair. Levi and Florence both gone, and all her children having to quit school one by one. But by morning she'd have her courage back, and put on a smile for the children, fixing them breakfast as they all went their separate ways.

Young Bertha always grumbled about whoever she was working for that day, but her Mom always whispered as she walked out the door, "Remember, Honey, God don't like ugly."

When she was out of her mother's hearing, Bertha would mutter back, "It's too bad, he don't like poverty either."

But Bertha didn't blame her mother for having to quit school. She knew how proud her mother was. Rather than accept charity, she have her children work. They'd still had good times together as a family and even before she and Bert had started working, they'd enjoyed their childhood days on Delaware Drive.

CHAPTER 7

Childhood Days

After school Bert, Bertha, Ella, Teddy, all of Logania's children discovered the delights of Delaware Drive. During the growing up years of her children, for various reasons, Logania had moved to six different houses on Delaware Drive. But access to the Delaware River was like a magic wand. In the summer there were daily swims in the Wilson Dam. Races over to the haunted Getter's Island were held every day. Playing on the island and diving in the river were a normal day's activities. With a few cookies and some lemonade, picnics were held every day in the old chicken shacks left on the College Hill woods from the past. They became clubhouses. Sometimes Logania would walk her brood to Eddyside, another beach where they could swim all day and later eat their sandwiches somewhere in the shade on the sand covered beach.

And Hurrah for the Bushkill Park Picnics. Even when I was born in 1943, they were still having them. Always on a Thursday, our Mom's day off, we'd go out early and ride the rides all morning. Then about 12:00 in the afternoon, Logania and all our Moms would come out on the trolley, bearing baskets of food. And such food, golden fried chicken, tangy potato salad, macaroni salad, baked beans, different kinds of cakes, fruit, just about everything. The children would fidget and jump around while the adults covered the picnic tables with newspapers and tablecloths and transform them into tables full of delights. Then we'd have our meal under the swaying trees, with the clanging sound of the rides calling us back, the humming of the bees as they caught the aroma of our feast. Then all day we'd ride returning to the food whenever we were hungry. Finally at night the Moms would pack everything up and sit under the quaint old carousel, listening to the music until the children were exhausted enough to go home, usually around twelve midnight. I wonder if my brother Wesley remembers always having to hold his big brother's Skeeter's hand so he wouldn't get lost, and then one time making a break for freedom to run off with the Hackett boys. Such was the joy of those picnics.

Then there were the winters. The end of Delaware Drive ran into Bushkill Drive where at the end of the street sat an enormous hill. In summer it was just a hill, but in winter covered with snow, it was a sledding dream. Any type of object that would slide was up for grabs. Can you still feel the icy air, the rush of adrenaline, as you sped down that hill at breakneck speed. The children spent hours sliding down that hill until darlcness fell, then walked home noses running, hands freezing, but exhilarated beyond belief.

At home, despite the slurs they suffered at school, Logania encouraged them to talk about their day, and for the most part, all her children and their children enjoyed their school years even though of all Logania's children only Rebecca, the youngest child was allowed to remain in school until graduation. She was the first, but then all the grandchildren that were born afterward all graduated from High School and many of them have gone on to graduate from college., and the great grandchildren are following in their footsteps. In our family we have nurses, teachers, PHD's who have landed extraordinary jobs, entertainers, policemen, window designers, computer wizards, and several writers. This is just in Logania's portion of the family. I'm sure all her brothers and sisters and their descendants have honors many also. So Ardelia had the right idea back in the slave days when she encouraged her children to learn everything they could, because her legacy lives on.

Before I go to talk about each of Logania's children, I'd like to give you some idea of what an extraordinary person my grandmother was. Delaware Drive where we lived was really a highway Route 611, on which cars whizzed by at amazing speeds. At one time a Lafayette student was picked to sit out in the cold opposite our house to clock the traffic. Our Logania watched him shiver and sit for a time and finally her gentle heart could no longer stand it. She searched the house and found an old rug he could sit on and wrap around him to keep warm. He never forgot her kindness.

Once a homeless white youth came up our street begging for food. Our Logania watched his slow painful progress up the street as door after door was slammed in his face. By the time he reached our door, he was shivering and red faced. When Logania opened the door he recoiled in surprise, not expecting a dark face to open the door.

Recovering, he said, "Mam, could you spare a bit of food?"

Logania smiled. "The Lord always provides for those who need it." she said. "But you look awful cold. Do you have anywhere to go tonight?"

She glanced at the ominous gray clouds overhead. "It looks like snow."

"No Mam, I really don't, but I'll find somewhere to go. If I could just have a bite to eat."

"You certainly can," said Logania, but you'll eat it at our table. Please come in."

The young man had meat loaf and mashed potatoes to eat that night and for the next two weeks slept behind Logania's stove on an old rug until he found a job and a place to stay. This in a two bedroom home with an attic that was already overloaded with Logania's own children. He never forgot the sweet colored lady that cared enough to feed him and give him a place to sleep either. One day after he'd gotten a job, he returned to give a bag of vegetables to the nice lady that helped him when he needed it. I, myself never saw my grandmother sit down and eat her own supper until everyone else had eaten. Such was the integrity of my grandmother.

CHAPTER 8

Bertha's Revenge

Bertha in her twenties was a beautiful girl. With her caramel colored skin and long wavy dark hair, she had a lot of young men who desired to go out with her. But Bertha had sworn she didn't want any man, after having watched her mother struggle so hard. That was until she met Steve.

Tall and dark, he was, handsome beyond words and most of all charming. People said he could charm a bird off a tree with that debonair manner of his. At any rate he convinced young Bertha to go out with him and she fell hopelessly in love with him. One evening when Bertha returned home, Logania said to her daughter.

"You know, Honey, what kind of reputation he has. Maybe you shouldn't take what he says seriously.

"Oh, Mom, I know what people say but he isn't like that. He really isn't. He wants to marry me. We have it all planned."

So though Logania had misgivings, Steve and Bertha were happily married and moved into an apartment, they could barely afford.

Not many months later Stephen Jr. was born, and Bertha was ecstatic. She loved this little replica of Steve so much, she feared to ever leave him alone. Little Stevie was about two when the rumors started. Steve returned home later and later at night and finally one night didn't return until morning. Bertha could no longer ignore the rumors after that.

Steve had a white mistress. Not only that, she was rich and very married. When Bertha confronted him, he never denied it.

"Long as I take care of little Stevie and pay the bills, I'll do what I want," he shouted.

"You conceited ape!! Don't you know your playing with fire?" Bertha retorted. "Just stay away from little Steve and I. We don't need you."

It was only a month later that a policeman came to Bertha's door one night.

He carried his hat, hemmed and hawed a bit, then finally said, "Mrs. Henley, your husband's been shot tonight. He was trying to rob Mrs. Grindel and her husband came home and killed him."

Bertha walked straight up to his face. "You and I both know he was not robbing that lady. The whole police force knows he's been messing with her for months. And you all are going to let that bastard get away with killing my husband in cold blood. Just another nigger, to you, right?"

The policemen said, "Look, lady, there's no call for that kind of language. I'm sorry." Then he walked away.

Bertha was so angry, she never took time to grieve her husband's death. The next day she told her mother what had happened.

'Mom, I'm going to make that woman sorry. That Jezebel. She could have stopped this.'"Now, Honey, don't go trying to punish her. Leave that to God. 'Vengeance is mine sayeth the Lord' You know I told you before God don't like ugly. We'll all help you arrange the funeral, and you find out about his insurance."

Bertha smiled slyly. "I've taken care of all that, Mom. But that insurance money aint gonna pay for his funeral. I'm giving it to you Mom, to help you."

"Honey, what do you mean? You have to use it for his funeral." Bertha just smiled. "Just let me take care of it, Mom, O.K.?"

The next morning Bertha dressed in her best hat and dress and took the trolley downtown to the rich section of town. Without any hesitation, she found the house she was looking for. When she knocked on the door, a young maid answered.

"Yes'," she said curiously.

Bertha said, "I'd like to speak to the mistress of the house.

"Do you have an appointment?" she said cautiously.

Bertha stepped forward. "I don't need an appointment. You can tell her Mrs. Henley is calling. I'm sure she'll know who I am."

Bertha watched understanding dawn in her eyes and then she took off at a run, leaving the door open, so Bertha walked in and sat down.

Immediately Mrs. Grindel appeared in a beautiful dress, three gold necklaces on her neck, and diamonds on her fingers. That dress alone would pay our rent for a year thought Bertha.

"What can I do for you, Mrs. Henley?" she said. You know you shouldn't be here. I could have you arrested."

"For stealing from you just like Steve, I suppose," said Bertha.

"Now, look," began Mrs. Grindel.

"NO, you look!" Bertha got up and paced so angry she couldn't sit still. "You know Steve wasn't robbing you. You and Steve have been sleeping together for months. There are even some questions about the parternity of your son. Your husband knows that too. What you're going to do is pay for his funeral. You owe him that at least."

"What?" Mrs. Grindel looked astonished. "I'm sure he has insurance. He told me he had a job."

Bertha advanced angrily. "I don't give a damn what he told you. You owe him this at least and if I don't get a check from you today, I'm going straight to the newspaper and this whole town will know your husband shot my husband because he was sleeping with you."

Sue Grindel stood up and picked up her purse. Very carefully she pulled out her checkbook and pen. She wrote a few lines and then looked up. "How much?'

"Well how much do you think a man's life is worth?" asked Bertha. "Even if he was just a nigger?"

Sue gasped. "Please," she said. "I'm sorry. I never meant for this to happen. How much do you want?"

"Three thousand should do it," said Bertha. "It's only gonna cost you three thousand for ruining a little boy's life and making me an angry bitter woman."

Sue wrote the check and handed it to Bertha. There were tears in her eyes. 'Im sorry," she said. "I know it can't ever change anything, but I'm very very sorry.

"One thing you taught me," said Bertha, is not to trust any man. I've learned a good lesson."

Then Bertha went home and told her Mom the story. "I think I should move back home," she said. I'll go back to work and help out again if you can watch little Stevie, and something else

Mom, I'm never going to trust a man again. If I see someone I favor I'll just live with him."

"What about the children?" asked her Mom.

"Children, there aren't going to be any more children. I have little Steve and he makes up for everything. And true to her word, Bertha met a lot more handsome men in her lifetime, may have even lived with some but she never married again.

CHAPTER 9

Bertella's Loves

After Bertella quit school, she worked long hard days for Mrs. Joseph but occasionally she and sister Bertha and a few friends would go out together. It was on one of these occasions, she met Charles Cherry and fell hopelessly and totally in love.

He was regally tall with light brown skin and dark mysterious eyes which set her heart aflutter. She and the girls were eating dinner before going to a movie when suddenly she spotted him at the opposite table. After that she kept sneaking glances at him, then looking away, when his glance met hers. He continued to watch her until Bertella finally gave up trying to eat.

Finally he got up and walked over to their table. I know this sounds forward, but I've been watching you all through dinner. You are beautiful. Bert looked down embarrassed, while her friends just giggled, but Bertha smacked her lips angrily.

The man bent closer. "Would you walk with me? I'll make sure you get home safely. I'm just a harmless Taylor.

Bertha whispered, "I'll tell Mom, Bert."

But Bertella never heard her. She was taking Charles outstretched hand, and together they left the restaurant. After that day, they were inseparable. Bert was in love. It wasn't long before they were planning a wedding.

"Well," Logania said, "We must get a wedding gown and get married in a church and—"

"No, Mom, we don't want all that. We can't afford it. We're going to use the money to get furniture for our apartment. We'll just say our vows before a justice of the peace.""Besides," Bert smiled shyly, "We really don't have time to plan all that."

Logania placed her hands on her hips. "Well, Honey, you really should get married in a church.

"But, Mom, I told you we don't have a lot of time."

"O.K., Honey, You have my blessing and I'll help in any way I can."

On August 24, 1924 Charles and Bertella stood before a justice of the peace with all the family present and promised to love, honor, and obey for life. The only concession they made was that Charles made Bert a beautiful wedding gown. She looked beautiful glowingly in love.

Later at a celebration supper at her Mom's house, Logania told them all the story of her famous wedding gown. Bertella laughed till she choked on her piece of chicken. Everyone had to tell a funny story then, and by the time Bert and her new husband walked across the street to their apartment, they were very happy and more in love than ever.

Bertella was having a baby. Any day now, those first warning pains would start and she would go to the hospital. She should be thrilled at the birth of her first child but she was very unhappy. Her husband even at this very moment languished with tuberculosis, desperately ill in the hospital. As if in sympathy with her thoughts, the baby twisted, and gut wrenching pain ripped through her middle. The little one was on his way, no matter if Daddy was O.K. or not.

First babies are always slow, she'd been told but this one seemed to be in a hurry. She and Charles were happy in the little apartment right up the street from her Mom's house until Charles's took sick. Now it was time to have her first baby and all she felt was sadness.

After the next grinding pain, she hurried out of the house, and over to her Mom's house. When Logania saw her daughter clutching her middle, she wasted no time in having one of the neighbors call an ambulance.

In the hospital, Bertella labored on with Logania beside her holding her hand. Maybe this baby knew it had to get here fast. When it looked like it was time, the nurse chased Logania away so Bertella, surrounded by nurses and doctors pushed young Charles Jr. into the world.

"Take us to his father," Bert whispered to the nurse. "He's on the fifth floor. He's very sick."

"I can't do that," answered the nurse.

"His father is dying of tuberculosis," Bertella said weakly. "Please, this may be his only chance to see his son."

"But you've just had a baby. That's not possible," argued the nurse. "Besides we can't allow a new born that close to a disease of that sort."

A young doctor with light brown hair and strange hazel eyes approached the nurse, "Take her up," he said.

"But" stammered the nurse.

"Take her," he said.

So they loaded the tired, weak, Bertella and the baby into a wheel chair and took them up to the fifth floor where his Daddy got a glimpse of his new born son, and a tearful kiss from his young wife just before he died at the ripe old age of twenty-six. The nurse was in hysterics after the kiss, but Bertella leaned close again and whispered, "Remember I'll always love you and our son looks just like you." Then the nurse wheeled them quickly away.

Always after that day, Bertella never knew whether to rejoice on that 15th day of January or mourn her loss, and so it was with mixed feelings she faced that month ever after.

Young Bertella returned home with her brand new son, disillusioned and bitter. A young woman of twenty, just starting to love, already a widow with a child to raise alone. Depressed and still weary from childbirth, she attended her husband's funeral with the rest of the family.

"Honey," her mother said as they left the cemetery, "You can move back in with me. You need some time to grieve and I can help watch little Charles."

So within a few days, young Bertella packed her belongings and moved back home. This way, Mom could watch the baby and she could return to work to pay off the accumulated bills.

One cold February night, Bertella sat on the stoop outside and gazed at the stars in the cold brilliant sky.

"God," she whispered. "Am I doomed to sorrow forever? I loved school so much and I was forced to quit. Reciting for the teachers was my greatest thrill, and I had to leave. I could write beautiful poems, but that's all gone. Now you've taken my Charlie and I have to return to cleaning some rich woman's dirt. Is this all that life has to offer me?"

In the stillness of the night, all she could hear was the wind whipping through the trees. If she listened very closely, it sounded like DON'T GIVE UP, BERT, NEVER GIVE UP. She shivered violently, then she whispered, "Thank you Charlie," and then quietly went in and went to bed.

Two years later it happened again. Bert, who swore she'd never go out again with any man ever again met a railroad porter. Bert was a dreamer and on one Saturday when she had a day off, she walked over to Canal Street where the railroad was to watch the trains to arrive and depart. Then she'd make up stories about the people she saw getting on and off the trains. On this particular day while she was sitting on one of the passenger benches daydreaming, a light skinned man in a porter uniform walked up to her.

"What town are you in right now?" he asked her smiling.

"Oh!" Bert jumped. "I was just daydreaming. Who are you?"

"Well," he said, "as you can see I'm a porter and I was just given a three day leave in this little town. Do you think a pretty young girl like you could show me the sights?'

Bert jumped up hurriedly. "I don't even know your name," she said.

He held out his hand. "Marien Wynne," he said shaking her hand. "Don't laugh," he said when she smiled. "That is really my name. Maybe that's why I'm a porter. I have to go where the wind takes me."

"Now," he said, "I'm starving. Would you know a nice place we could have lunch together."

"There is the Monoplane Restaurant over on Third Street, but I barely know you."

"I promise I won't attack you while we're eating lunch," and then he flashed a beautiful smile.

So Bertella had lunch with Marien and they talked about the places he'd traveled. She found herself fascinated by him. So when he suggested going back to his room, which he rented in Center Square, Bert never hesitated. She could hear her Mom saying it's not proper, Bert, but still she went anyway. She wanted to hear more stories. On the way Marien stopped and bought a bottle of wine and fruit and cheese. Much later that afternoon, Marien was helping her button her dress, and Bert knew she'd done it again. She'd fallen in love with a total stranger.

Marien took both her hands in his. "Don't, Bert," he said. "Don't be ashamed. Your the sweetest young girl I've met in a long time. I really care about you. I really do. Now I'm going to take you home, but I want to see you again. Do you think your parents would let me take you to church? Could we spend the day together tomorrow?"

Bert knew she should stay home to help with the chores, and care for the children, but she was young and in love, so of course she chose the day with Marien What a wonderful day it was.

In church the other girls jealously wondered where Bert found this handsome young man. He talked to no one but Bert. After church he rented a boat, and took her for a long ride down the Delaware River. It was mid July and the day was perfect. Birds chirped and twittered as they floated by, now and then a fish would leap out of the water causing gentle ripples, soft breezes whispered through the trees causing the leaves to twist restlessly overhead. Bert leaned back, closed her eyes and just relaxed enjoying the pleasant hum as all the sounds blended together. She was almost asleep, when she felt two warm lips touch her own. That woke her up quickly.

"You looked so pretty, I couldn't resist," said Marien "How bout we pull over there and rest in the shade a bit?"

Bert agreed, and she wasn't a bit surprised to see Marien had brought along a blanket. They spread it in a secluded beach area, and soon they forgot everything except each other. Later, Marien even talked her into swimming, though they had no bathing suits, and though Bert insisted on keeping her underwear on, she had to admit she enjoyed herself immensely.

Later as they were rowing back, and Bert was frantically trying to dry her hair with a blanket, Marien said, "Bert, can I see you tomorrow? I only have one more day here."

Bert shook her head. "You know I have to work. As it is since you've been here I've neglected my son, and left Mom with all the work to do."

All right, where do you work, Bert?" he asked.

"I work on College Hill for Mrs. Joseph, but why do you want to know?"

"You'll see," he said with a smile. "Just relax. You should relax more. Today you look like a young girl in love and very happy, and that's how you should always look."

The next day right at lunch time, the doorbell rang at the home of Mrs. Joseph where Bert was working. It was Marien and he was carrying a basket again.

"You can't come in here," gasped Bert.

"Why not?" he said with a smile. "No one is home but you."

"I know, but if Mrs. Joseph finds out, I could be fired," said Bert looking around to see if anyone was watching.

"Look Honey, we're not going to do anything but have lunch. You're allowed to do that, right?

Well then, eat your lunch and I'll just watch."

Bert got out the lemonade and made them both a sandwich and they talked some more. Bert'd never met anyone who knew so much about so many different things. She loved talking to him. When they finished eating, Marien asked now what do you have to do?"

"I have to clean the bedrooms, straighten the children's room, and clean the bathrooms."

"Give my some cleaners, and show me where the bathrooms are."

"What?" gasped Bert.

"I'm going to help you clean," he said.

An hour later, he found Bert just finishing the children's room. She smiled at him. "Tired already?"

"No," be said, "I want you to check my work."

Bert followed him from bathroom to bathroom. They were all spotless.

"Now," he said, "since it seems your finished for the day, we can go have our picnic."

"But," said Bert.

He smiled at her. "Is everything done?"

"Yes, but—"

"Doesn't she leave you your money when she is not here?"

"Yes, but"

"But, but, but, come on Bert, get your money and let's go. We have all afternoon for our picnic for tonight I have to leave."

They walked down the lane and through the woods climbing through bushes and trees until they found a little clearing all surrounded by forest. It was there they had their picnic. Bert didn't know it but it was the same spot,

Levi and Logania found so many years ago. They spent all afternoon talking and loving each other.

Finally Bert said, "your leaving tonight?"

"I have to," Marien answered, "but don't you worry. I'll be back. I haven't met anyone like you ever before. I'm going to try to get a permanent job around here, but I have to leave with the train tonight."

"I don't even know your address," whispered Bert.

"I live in Boston, Honey. I don't have anything to write with right now but I'll write to you, Bert, I promise. I know your address. I wrote it down the first day I met you. Expect to hear from me by next Saturday at the latest. I promise I'll be back. I need someone like you in my life."

Slowly they walked down the lane holding hands. When they reached the point where the trolley usually stopped, they found little Skeeter waiting.

"Mommy, Mommy, your home early," he cried running to hug her.

"Cute little guy," Marien said, patting him on the head. "If you can carry this picnic basket home for Mommy, you can have everything in it."

"Oh, boy, I can carry it all right," Skeeter yelled. Then he ran on ahead carrying the leftover food.

Bert and Marien walked slower, still talking about when they would see each other again. Finally when they reached her house, Marien pressed into her hand the ring he wore on his pinkie finger.

"It's not an engagement ring," he whispered, "but it's a promise."

Then he quickly walked away before Bert could see the tears in his eyes or he could see hers.

Months passed without a word from him and the next March, her little boy was born. Bertella was so ashamed of her unmarried state that when she felt the first labor pains, she refused to go to the hospital. Logania pleaded with her but she was adamant. Finally Logania persuaded a doctor to come to the house and deliver the little boy. When the baby was placed in her arms, Bertella saw him only as another one of the failures of her life. This sweet innocent baby was hers, but all she felt was emptiness. She thought angrily of his father. I have to go where the wind takes me he'd told her. Well, the wind had taken him west, so she named her baby Wesley. Listlessly, she continued her life taking care of the baby only when her Mom reminded her. One evening while bathing her son, she dropped him into the water where he almost drowned. Snatching him to safety, she finally realized how much she loved her Wesley. She was so young, but she truly loved her two little boys. She never knew why Marien didn't return and she left husband less but after that she tried to do better with her boys and she stayed away from men entirely for the next five years. One day she did hear of a horrible crash, one of the trains he rode, that happened just outside of Boston, but she never knew for sure.

—

CHAPTER 10

Ella

Ella was born in 1908, and as I mentioned earlier, suffered many bouts of illness. She begged Logania to stay home with her and take care of baby Teddy. She really did not want to go to school. Then fate stepped in and intervened.

One morning Ella woke complaining of a stomach ache. Logania fed her weak tea and ministered to her all day, but Ella's stomach ache worsened hour by hour. Finally Logania took her young daughter to the hospital.

Sitting in the waiting room with her other children, Logania reflected on what a hard year it had been. She'd just been in the hospital herself having her son Theodore, and had made up her mind there weren't going to be any more children, and now here was Ella seriously ill. Was this her punishment for not wanting any more children? This was a trying year. One of the worst for keeping the kids clothed and fed. Now she sat with Teddy in her arms surrounded by her other children. They all looked frightened. Young Bertella, who was only ten, kept sniffling. Bertha kept hold of Richard who was about five. The waiting room was quiet except for Bert's sniffles. Logania rocked little Teddy and prayed. The doctors looked awful grim when they'd taken Ella away.

"Mommy, she's gonna be all right, isn't she? asked Bertha.

"I don't know, Honey," whispered Logania. "All we can do is pray."

Down at the end of the corridor, the doors swished open and closed. Everyone looked up expectantly. It was Levi, striding towards them who'd just been told.

"How is she?" he asked as he lifted young Richard to his knee.

"No one's been back to tell us," whispered Logania.

As if out of nowhere a doctor appeared in front of them. Logania knew. Before he even spoke, she could tell by the way his eyes never met hers directly.

"I'm sorry," he said. "Her appendix burst. We did all we could do."

"Oh no," yelled Levi. "Not my daughter. She was just fine two days ago. What kind of hospital is this?'

A couple of nurses passing by looked smpathetically at them but kept walking. Logania stood up wearily, her eyes full of tears."

"Come, Levi," she said. "Yelling at the doctors won't bring our Ella back."

"Can we see her?' she said quietly to the doctor.

"Of course," he said. "But the children?"

"Bertha, you keep them all together," Logania said. "I'll take Teddy with me. Levi and I want to tell our Ella good-bye."

When they reached the room, there were so many machines and tubes around, they could barely see their little girl. There in the midst of a sea of white lay a still little brown face. Logania bent down and kissed her sweet face.

"Sweet Baby," she whispered. "You'll never have to go to school, now. Your going straight to Heaven to be with God. I guess he needed another angel."

Levi just bent over and kissed her forehead and then quickly exited the room.

They had to ride the trolley home. Bert sniffled all the way home while Bertha muttered angrily about no good doctors. Levi simply patted Logania's back. There were no words that could take away her pain.

Ella was buried in Easton Cemetery on a cold, cloudy day with all her brothers and sisters present. Logania's relatives in Charlottesville couldn't attend the funeral but they sent a letter which Bertha read to her.

Dear Logania,

I know how hard this must be for you. But remember to keep your belief in God and one day you'll understand his taking Ella. I hope the money we sent will help with expenses.

Love from Pa, and all your brothers and sisters.

CHAPTER 11

Bertella's Loves Cont.

Even though Bertella never knew for sure what happened to Marien, she decided to stay away from anymore romances indefinitely. She had little free time, as she was usually exhausted after a day of cleaning. She'd eat supper and then fall tiredly into bed. She loved her two little boys but spent little time with them. It was Logania who in the evenings had the whole family tell stories about the days events and sometimes entertain each other. Charles (who was immediately nicknamed Skeeter) could sing. Stephen, Bertha's little boy would play drums on anything that made a sound, and young Wesley would watch them and wish that he could shrug off the slurs of the day as easily as his brother. It was decided when they reached school age that Skeeter and Stephen would attend March School on College Hill.

Bertella remembered her years at McCartney School. Now her son was attending a rich all white school and the family still poor. She could imagine the insults they would endure. But amazingly, like young Bertha, they did remarkably well. Both young Skeeter and Stephen were on the football and basketball teams. They were still so poor that young Skeeter had to wear Teddy's old shoes to school. Stephen, also suffered the same misfortune, but when they were called names, they had a ready answer and then simply ignored the perpetrators. Because the two boys did so well in sports, they soon gained popularity despite the color of their skins and their apparent poverty. Stephen eventually won the American Legion Award, the highest award given by March School to any student black or white.

When Wesley started school, he started late in the year, stacking the odds against him even more. He attended Taylor School in faded used clothes and two big shoes and suffered endless teasing by his classmates. Like his mother his feelings were easily hurt by the slurs.

Even some of his teachers treated him unfairly but with the odds stacked against him Wesley persevered. He went on to graduate from school, did a stint in The Air Force, and eventually graduated from College. A determined young man who accomplished miracles.

Bertella, meanwhile felt her youngest son's pain but did not know what to do to make things better. Other than working every day to earn money to make things easier, she was at a loss at what to say to him.

Often in the silence of the night, she would pray to wake up suddenly rich, thinking that would fix all her problems. When she'd bitterly complain to her Mom, her Mom would say in that gentle way of hers, "Honey, we reap what we sow. If you feel bitter and frustrated and defeated all the time, then that's what you'll attract in your life."

Maybe that's why when a gentlemen came along, with the odd name of Bunny Steele who could make his banjo sing. A good time man out to have fun, she was ripe to be attracted to him. Bert was long overdue for some fun. She started going out drinking with Bunny and dancing over in Phillipsburg, NJ, things she'd never done before. Unlike Bertha who was the love em and leave em type, Bert always gave her heart right away. Eventually she fell in love with Bunny too, even though she'd been told by everyone, he was just a good time man.

When Bunny learned Bert was pregnant, he packed his banjo and loped back across the bridge to leave Bert to handle the consequences alone. Knowing she'd been warned about his character, Bert pretended to the world that she didn't care, but her tender heart was broken once again.

In March 1934, Bert delivered her first little girl. To see that sweet, tiny face made up for all the anguish she'd suffered and she understood that her Mom's policy of life was the right one.

Logania never complained, never cried at least not in front of the children, she always had a kind word and a loving hug when someone needed it, and no one ever went hungry in her presence. Here was a woman who'd taken care of her brothers and sisters, her mother, came all the way to Easton to care for someone else's child, had taken care of all her own children and her husband, and now she was caring for all the grandchildren with never an angry or impatient word. in fact, everyone called her Mom for she was like a Mom to all of us.

"Mom, they must've broken the mold after they made you," Bertella'd say often to her mother. When young Margie started school, she was timid also but she soon made lots of friends and her teachers loved her willing attitude and soon she was excelling in all subjects.

Little Margie, was timid also like her mother, but she made lots of friends on Delaware Drive, and went to March School for a short time also. She had to wear second hand clothes just as the others, and endured the slurs of her classmates. With her close group of friends though, she began to enjoy school and accepted the life on Delaware Drive. Margie had a beautiful singing voice and a talent for drawing and her pleasant personality pleased all of her teachers.

After Margie's birth, Bert made up her mind to just enjoy the children she had, and help take care of her mother and younger sister Rebecca, but the best laid plans of mice and men never work as we all know. Bert thought her child bearing years over, and looked forward now to a quiet life taking care of her children and her mother.

Bertella at thirty eight was a good looking woman. She had one of those faces that look perpetually young when a handsome well dressed man and his brother came to Easton from New Jersey, all the Mills girls were attracted. Bert claimed she wasn't, but whenever sister Bertha talked about them, she had to hear every word.

"The dark skinned one looks like an Indian," Bertha whisper to Bert at night, "And I hear they want to settle in Easton."

"Why would anyone want to settle in Easton?" Bert asked.

"I hear he's an upholster and he wants to set up a shop, but he's so handsome with that straight black hair and he dresses like a model."

"Well," answered Bert, "No more men for me. I've learned my lesson. I don't care how cute he is."

"I hear the brother is very cute too," continued Bertha. "He's light skinned but wow is he cute."

"I don't want to hear anymore about it," whispered Bert, but as she closed her eyes she kept picturing a dark skinned man with Indian shaped features.

All the unattached black woman in Easton were infatuated with these two new handsome men, and they appeared to be well off money wise, but the person the dark skinned man asked out whose name was Bill by the way, was Bertha.

One evening when Bill walked Bertha home, Bert was sitting on the stoop watching Margie and her friend Madie play jump rope.

"Hello," he said. "How come I've never seen you before?"

"Oh, she never goes anywhere," said Bertha. "She doesn't want anything to do with men, anymore."

"Why not?" he asked, sitting down on the stoop next to Bert.

Bert looked up at him. God, he was handsome just as Bertha described him.

"I'm too old to be gallivanting about," answered Bert. "I've had my fun."

"What if I asked you to gallivant with me," he said.

"Oh don't mind me, Just make a date with my sister right in front of me, "Bertha said, but she was smiling.

"Well, Bert," said Bill, "Your sister doesn't mind."

"If my sister doesn't mind, then I guess I have no choice. I'd love to go out with you. Bert said Now I don't really what became of the light skinned brother, but the dark skinned one eventually became my father. Yes, my mother almost at the change of life stage was chosen by this debonair man and this one seemed perfect in every way. First he dressed as if he was an ad for the well dressed man. Because of his mixed parentage, his hair was straight and black, he was intelligent, an accomplished cook, and an upholster by trade. Most of all, he wanted to marry my mother. After her first ill fated marriage, and her two fickle suitors, Bert was being very cautious.

But not cautious enough for she fell in love with my father. On July 12, 1943,1 entered the world. 6lbs. 8ozs. of bouncing baby girl. This time as Bert struggled to bring me into the world, my father sat on one side, a sweet Irish nurse on the other. When it was time for me to be born, they chased my father out as they did back in those days and let him back when I was cleaned up and placed in my mother's arms. How different from the other births this must've been. My father wasn't sick upstairs, or absent by choice, or in parts unknown. He sat right there beside her holding Mom's hand and me.

"What should we name her?" he whispered. "She's beautiful."

Just at that moment the little nurse appeared. "Faith and Begorrah", she said. "Such a lovely Colleen, with that dark straight hair and those big brown eyes, and light skin, she almost looks Irish."

After she left, my Mom said, "She's been really good to me, that nurse, and she has such a lovely name, Eileen. Why don't we name her after her. After all, my Mom laughed, "we've just been told she looks Irish."

My Dad smiled. "Eileen, it is then, but her last name is going to be Hoffman, not Cherry. She's my child and I want the world to know that. She's going to have everything she wants in life and so are you. Your family has suffered enough."

So I was named Eileen Cherry Hoffman and later when I was christened, Sept. 16th, 1944 in Saint John's Rectory by Henry Comehlson Jr. with my mother and father standing by and I became the first of Bert's children not to suffer the sting of poverty and the last child she ever had. Often we'd visit my half white grandmother who owned a house in Flemington, New Jersey.

I'm sure my mother was tempted to marry my father and try to forget the years of poverty, but there was something about this wonderful woman, Logania, that caused all her children to remain as close to her as they could possibly be.

When I was first born, they may have lived together, and though Bert was offered the chance to be a wife and be taken care of, she opted to stay with her mother. sweet, patient, Logania who was getting up in years and had suffered various bouts of illness which caused the whole family to worry.

All the children were gone now except Teddy who sacrificed much to work and care for his mother, and Bertha who still worked everyday, but now divided her time between Mom and her grandchildren. Young Rebecca, newly married had a husband who had to remind her constantly, he needed her attention as much as her mother.

Bertella faced with the choice of leaving her Mom alone much of the time, while Bertha and Ted worked, chose not to marry, but to remain at home with

Logania and to spend only weekends with my Bill. A brave decision for one who only wanted a happy marriage her entire life. My father, being the proper man he was, legally adopted me so there would never be any doubt I was his daughter and Bert remained with him until he died in February 1956. Bertella was known as his common law wife and I his only child.

Now as we all know, there is no one without faults and my mother found out William E. Hoffman wasn't perfect either. He was a drinker and once in a bar, drank sometimes until he passed out. On many cold nights My Uncle Teddy brought him home to Logania's home to keep him from falling down and freezing on someone's doorstep, though he had a trade, a handsome face, a caring manner, and his own home.

Every weekend my Mom and I spent this time with him and my mother finally had someone care for her in the way she needed, until his persistent drinking caused his own illness and eventually his death.

When I reached school age, I attended kindergarten in St. John's Church, my father's decision, I'm sure and later Taylor School. I did very well in school also. but unlike my tender hearted mother and sister, I inherited a temper from my father and was questioned often of being Margie's sister as I had a sharp and ready tongue, especially when I felt I was being treated unjustly. So I was the result of my mother's last and final love, and though she suffered some serious bouts of illness during the time she spent with my father, I do believe that most of those years were happy.

CHAPTER 12

Life On The Block

Once a week the ice man would come lugging his huge hunk of ice that Mom placed in the top of the ice box. Then everyday, one of the children's job's was to empty the drip pan underneath as it melted.

Another one of the small excitements was when the vegetable lady came. Every week like clockwork, the vegetable lady came with her wagon load of fresh produce. Such fervor with everyone shouting to Logania to buy this and buy that. Loaded on the cart were bright, red, tomatoes, emerald green lettuce, huge cabbages, golden yellow corn, ripe bananas and even watermelon, a welcome treat. There was always a treat or two for the youngest, and then Logania and all the children would carry the load to the house rejoicing in the sheer happiness of fresh food for the coming week.

Every Christmas, Logania always made sure they had a tree, so one Christmas Eve when she discovered she didn't have enough money left to buy a tree, she was in despair. There had never been a Christmas without some type of tree. Suddenly a knock on the door and her neighbor from across the street, Mrs. Huse came in. She glanced sympathetically at the empty table in the corner where the tree usually sat.

"Mrs. Mills", she said, "1 know it's pretty late, but I just wanted to let you know our ice man, Tony, is selling Christmas trees at Riverside Park for a quarter since it's so close to Christmas."

"Thank you, for letting me know", Logania answered with a smile, "but I don't know if the boys can go all the way over there so late."

"Well", Mrs. Huse stood up. "I just wanted to tell you. Now, I have to get back to wrapping my presents."

After she'd left, Skeeter said, "Mom, can we go get one?"

"Yeah, I'll go with him, Mom. I'll help", called Steve.

Bobby, who'd been reading by the stove said, "I'll take them, Mom."

Logania looked sadly into her empty purse. Not even a penny. Skeeter followed her glance.

"It's O.K., Mom. We can buy the tree, Steve and I. Mr. Williams paid us for helping him fix that roof yesterday. Steve and I have enough to get a tree."

Mr. Williams, a master craftsman, worked in gardening, building, sort of a jack of all trades. He moved in with My Aunt Bertha and of course, his contribution helped with the never ending bills. Once in a while he hired the boys to help him and paid them ten cents each time, a small fortune at their age. Logania smiled. "You sure the two of you can carry a big tree by yourself."

"You bet we can," shouted Skeeter.

"O.K." she said, and the boys took off.

In ten minutes, they were back lugging a beautiful tree. That evening, everyone made something to go on the tree. Logania even popped corn, which they strung on thread and hung on the tree.

Later on, when the children were asleep, Logania put out the few parcels she wrapped in private. It was a mighty meager pile, now that she'd put it out. Bertha came down and put a few things under the tree, and then Bertella brought her things down. It had been a hard year. Her wrapped packages only contained new socks for the boys and a pair of shoes for Margie who was just starting to walk. Her eyes met her Mothers over the small pile of presents.

"No toys again, Mom?" she said. "It isn't fair. They don't understand why Santa Claus never makes it here. We can't use that no snow excuse again."

"I know it's hard, Honey, but at least we have a tree. It wouldn't seem like Christmas without a tree."

"Yes, one they had to buy themselves. Mom, it's not fair. Where are the toys the Salvation Army brings?"

Logania shook her head. "I don't know. It's been a bad year all over. We'll just have to tell them something."

"What about Rebecca? She knows there's no Santa Claus. She's a young girl. She wants pretty things to wear to school." "Rebecca will understand," answered Logania.

"Oh, Mom, it doesn't work that way when your young. She'll be just as disappointed as the rest. Well, Mom I'm going to bed. Don't stay up too late."

Then Bertella reached out and gave her Mom a big hug. "I know none of this is your fault," she whispered.

Logania sat down in her favorite old green chair and looked at the tree the boys decorated so lovingly. She was just drifting off to sleep when she heard a loud knock on the door. Startled, Logania looked out the peephole before opening the door since it was almost twelve. She recognized the young man from college who she'd given the rug to keep warm and he was carrying a bag of gifts.

When Logania opened the door he smiled, "Got some things for you. I think you can use."

Out of his bag he pulled a shiny red fire engine, a baseball bat and ball, a little girl's Mickey Mouse watch, a shiny drum, several boxes of candy, and several men's scarves. Carefully, he stacked the gifts around the tree, and then he approached Logania.

"And for this sweet lady," he said, "the only one on this street that cared if I froze or not, this is to keep you warm."

He handed Logania a beautiful white knitted scarf, long enough to wrap around her neck several times. Logania was weeping.

"God bless you, Son," she said. This was going to be one sad Christmas but you've made it the happiest we've had in a long time."

Then Logania said a little thank you prayer and finally went to bed.

The next morning no one but Logania knew what had happened and even her older children convinced that Santa Claus had come, and though Bertha pestered her about what really happened that night, Logania never told.

It's obvious that despite the poverty, the family suffered and hardships they went through, there were good times too.

Later when I was born, and Margie and Skeeter and Wesley were still at home, we would put on whole plays to entertain our Mom and Logania Mills. Margie and Skeeter could sing. Wesley and I acted out the parts. Soon after though, both Wesley and Skeeter went into the service, but I still remember the laughter when we all got together to entertain our Moms.

Chapter 13

Robert

Robert was born in 1916, one year after Teddy at a time when Logania was at a vulnerable stage in her life. She'd just lost young Ella to appendicitis. Her faith was greatly shaken.

The night Robert was born, Logania was in labor twenty-four hours straight, as if by sheer will power, she could keep another young life from entering this world to suffer. When the child was finally born, he was the tiniest of any of her children. But when he opened his eyes, Logania was startled by the depth she saw in them. He had clear brown, beautiful eyes, but this tiny baby looked at her as if he knew all about her inner pain. When she mentioned this to Levi, he just laughed.

"Nonsense, Honey, That's impossible. He's just a baby like the rest, maybe a little tinier, that's all."

Young Bobby, though was different than the rest. When the other's would go swimming as a group or play up and down Delaware Drive, Bobby could never be found. Usually someone would go searching for him at dinner time to find him studying an earthworm in the yard or sitting under a tree watching the birds.

Skeeter loved his Uncle Bobby because he would tell him the most amazing stories. He seemed to know about everything and even surpassed Bertella in his eagerness to read. Mrs. Joseph, who Bertella worked for, gave Bert one Christmas, a copy of Gone With The Wind as a gift Both Bert and young Bobby read the book over and over until it lost both covers and a couple of pages. One evening when they sat on the stoop watching the stars, he told Skeeter one day men would walk on the moon.

"Uncle Bobby, that's never gonna happen." Skeeter laughed. "There's no air up there."

"Oh, they'll wear space suits with masks that carry their own supply of air, and you know what, a black man's going to make it possible."

Bobby was right although he never knew it, for in 1940 in a study known as Project Diana, an African-American named Walter S. McAfee, a mathematician calculated the speed of the moon. Without these calculations, Americans would have never walked on the moon, although McAfee was never recognized for his work until now.

Bobby often told Skeeter that one day in the White House, there would be a black man wearing a white shirt and black suit. Although Skeeter didn't believe a lot of the tales, his Uncle Bobby told him, he enjoyed talking to him and listening because everything he said was fascinating.

Bertella' d often tell her brother Bobby to stop filling her sons heads with fantasies, Bertella, at this point in her life, had made some bad decisions, and had lost some of her belief in the happy ever after dream Later on though she apologized to Bobby when she saw some of his predictions starting to take form. As we know today, Bobby who was far ahead of his time, was right in every story he told Skeeter.

Of all Logania's children, he was the most comforting. He seemed to have an inborn sense of knowing when she felt her lowest, for he was always there with a big hug and a smile when she was feeling her worse.

"It'll be all right, Mom," he'd whisper, and Logania'd be astonished for she sought to hide any sadness she felt from her children.

When he started school, the teachers had little patience with him as be seldom answered a question or even paid attention in class. His attention would be focused on a butterfly on the window sill or the angle of the sun. When he did speak, he'd say strange things about the future of the black race, which irritated all but a few of his teachers. Some called him retarded as often he'd be spoken to and wouldn't respond.

Later, though, he'd tell his mother, "Mom, I didn't answer because she treated me with disrespect. We are both equal, she and I. I deserve as much respect as she."

As Logania agreed with him, she'd usually only say, "Bobby, just try to pass the class. I know how you really feel, but we colored folk are still not taken seriously, and all we can do is try to adapt. We are doing a little better, you know, my mother was a slave. Just try Bobby."

Bobby continued though in his own way, experimenting in the yard, telling young Wesley and Skeeter unbelieving tales about the future. One day young Bobby got up, went into the kitchen and filled a glass with a little water and a lot of salt and drank it. There after every day, he'd drink this concoction often, sometimes three times a day.

Mom was always buying salt. At this point in time salt hadn't been iodized yet. Yet Bobby drank it daily as if he needed it to survive. Indeed, Bobby was developing a goiter, and somewhere in that marvelous brain of his, knew salt had something in it that would help him. Finally a swelling developed in his throat and continued to grow day by day. Logania forced him to go to the hospital.

He protested, he didn't like doctors and despite their best efforts, Bobby died from his goiter June 1936.

On one of Loganias visits, Bobby whispered to her, "Don't grieve for me, Mom, like you did Ella. This is not a happy time for me. As you grow older, you'll see all the things I talked about and one day, Mom, you'll never have to worry about money again. You'll live in a beautiful house with a real bathroom, and you'll have dozens of grandchildren who will love and adore you."

In fact everyone will love you."

"Bobby, please, just rest and get better," pleaded Logania but Bobby died.

Another funeral, with all the children and now grandchildren weeping over Bobby's grave. No one could understand why Bobby died, as he had such a strong belief in a happier future.

Much later after Logania recovered from some of her grief, one of the doctors told her that if all that salt he'd eaten had been iodized, it would've cured the goiter. At that time they weren't iodizing the salt yet, but Bobby had known with some inner wisdom what his body needed to cure his condition.

After Bobby's death, Logania lost another child, Florence who we've discussed earlier in this book. Florence died in the womb and I'm sure Logania thought her to be the last. Logania did a great deal of praying at this stage of her life. There were so many tragedies happening so close together, she feared losing her faith. Then she'd remember Bobby's words, his prediction of a happy future, and she visibly gathered up her faith, drew on her strength from God, and went on with her life.

Chapter 14

Richard

The fourth of Logania's children born was Richard, two years after Ella. Young Richard, the entertainer, always with a ready smile, a song to sing, a joke to play on someone. Born with music in his soul, from the age of one he'd sit humming and playing tunes on his toy xylophone. Bertha'd try to get him to play school with Bert and Ella but Richard couldn't sit still long enough to play their games. In the middle of a lecture on the ABC's, he'd jump up and start playing a tune on a rock nearby.

Bertha'd cast him out of her little school group in disgust, but Richard would just walk away humming and still tapping out his tunes. He kept everyone entertained in the family, and probably was the first one to start the family plays.

When he reached school age, his light hearted attitude made him lots of friends. He went to school singing his own private tunes and drumming away on anything that made a good sound. When he came upon his sisters at school, he'd always have a ready joke to play on them. Bert would duck into a room every time she saw him coming, but Bertha strayed into his path purposely. She loved their confrontations, because she usually won.

Richard wasn't an athlete like his brother Ted but he loved music. He'd sit and compose whole songs in his head. He dreamed of playing in a band and being a star on stage. In the evening plays at night, Rich was the life of the party. In fact, Richard did get to play in a band called 'Ralph White Night Hawks'. A dream come true for him.

Later on when he reached High School, he came home one day wearing the red and white uniform of the Easton High Band. The family rejoiced. Richard's heart thumped as loud as his drum when he marched out on the field, the only black player in the band. How proud the family was of him. The family was sure he was definitely the best drum player there ever was.

"Except me, of course," Stephen'd say smiling.

Now at nights, they play duets.

But the never-ending problem of the household took over again. No money and Richard was forced to quit school like the rest to support the family. Good bye to the Night Hawks and The Easton Band and his dreams of fame. He took a job working on the New Bridge. He stuck with it for a year or so but with his exuberant personality, this wasn't for him.

At this time President Franklin Roosevelt started a program called The National Recovery Administration, an organization to reorganize industry and agriculture under government regulation. Richard saw it as an escape from the drudgery of his job and a way to still earn money. He joined the Civilian Conservation Core and was stationed in Camp Wyomissing, Pa. When his stint was up, and Rich returned home, his brother Teddy had quit school too. By this time he was quite bored with his job at the foundry. Both young boys were at a time in their life when they were sick of being poor, and the boredom of an uninteresting job, so they were ripe for the trouble that lay ahead.

During the mid thirties, right around the time of The Great Depression when people were desperate for money and any type of entertainment to lift up their spirits, a group of gangsters settled in Easton in the old barn on Delaware Street which use to be the ice house. They used it to keep barrels of beer and horses. They also took over a building on Pine Street where they ran a baudy house. They talked the boys, Teddy and Richard, into delivering messages back and forth between the two illegal operations.

The little money that they made could not make up for the wall of guilt that crushed their spirits every time they faced their Mom. Richard, so lively and high spirited, most of his life, now slunk around despondent and sad all the time.

One night in bed, he told Teddy, "Teddy, I'm not going to do it anymore. I'm not delivering anymore messages. We're hurting people and I can't even look Mom in the face?"

Teddy whispered back, "Rich, these men are gangsters. They're not going to just let us quit. You know that. I don't like doing it either."

"What can we do?" cried Richard. "When I was in the C.C.C., I felt proud because I was doing something useful for the country, but this. I feel like a criminal."

Teddy whispered back, "I know, Rich but you don't tell these guys, no. I can't look Mom in the eye either."

"Well, I am," answered Richard. "I'm telling em I'm not delivering any more messages and I'm doing it tomorrow."

Richard did exactly what he promised. The next day, he walked into that old barn where two cruel looking men sat playing cards.

"I quit," said Richard, "I can't do this to my mother. I can't live with this guilt everyday."

One of the guys laughed coarsely.

The one called Sal said, "when the boss hears about this, you'll be lucky to be living at all. Nobody quits on him."

Richard eyed nervously the bulge under his jacket and then turned and walked out leaving the package he was supposed to deliver that night lying on the table. All the way home, his legs were shaking, but he never looked back.

Two days later, Teddy and Richard were swimming at Eddyside.

"Maybe their not going to do anything," It's been two days," Richard said, as they started the long walk home.

Suddenly out of nowhere, a huge black car came speeding straight at Richard.

"Run!!!!!!!" screamed Teddy.

But the car now cruising at top speed, crashed into Richard slamming him against an electric pole. Somewhere, a lady screamed and Teddy could feel tears falling down his cheeks as he watched his brother crumple to the ground all bloody and torn up, and the huge black car sped away.

Someone must've called an ambulance, but all Teddy could remember was seeing his brother lying there broken and still as he bent over him crying. The next thing he remembered was sitting in a screaming ambulance as it whisked them to the nearest hospital, where they hurried Richard off to emergency, but Teddy saw the looks on their faces. He'd seen that look before when his sister Ella died.

One of the nurses must've called Logania, because after Teddy gave his name and his brother's name and their address, he sat numb in the waiting room, barely breathing. When he saw his mother, flanked by Bertha and Bertella, he dissolved again into tears.

"What happened, Teddy? Logania cried, "Why would those men do this?"

Teddy simply sobbed and Logania knew. For money, they'd done something for money, and now another one of her children lay dying while she waited in this hated sterile waiting room.

When a doctor finally appeared, Logania looked up hopefully.

"I'm not going to lie to you, Mrs. Mills," said Dr. Jackson. "It's bad, very bad. Richard is on the critical list. I don't expect him to make it. You might want to come and speak to him before—Logania stood once again in that cold, white hospital room, staring down at her pale faced son, surrounded by tubes and machines and bottles, the only sound the monotonous sound of the monitors as they ticked away his life. He was so still.

"Please, God," she whispered. "Don't take my Richard. Forgive him for what he's done, but he doesn't deserve to die.

Bertha who'd came in behind her said, "No it's the monsters in that car that deserve to die, but they'll go unpunished while we suffer, just like my Stephen's killer is living his life unpunished.

Bertella walked over and softly touched Richard's forehead.

"Please don't die, Rich," she said. "You're the life of the house. You can't die, Honey. Please wake up."

He lay so still swathed in bandages from head to toe. Bertella bent down, kissed his forehead, and moved back to a corner in the room where she could wipe her tears in privacy. Why did these rooms always look gray and dreary despite the abundance of white everywhere?

A nurse came in and adjusted some unknown liquids dripping into Richard's arm, and then glided silently out on those rubber soled shoes they always wear. Outside the closed door, she wiped a stray tear from her own eye. She'd known Rich in school. He'd been a good friend, all that vibrancy, she thought, reduced to this. A doctor walked by eyeing her strangely. so she hurried off to complete her rounds. But later on when she had a short break, she whispered a prayer for Richard in the hospital chapel.

Bobbie came rushing in the room still out of breath from his hike from the trolley. He stood looking at his brother for a long time and then finally said, "Mom, he's going to make it. I feel that he will make it."

He looked carefully around the room and gave a little shiver, "But"

"But what, Bobby?" asked Logania

"Nothing, Mom, I feel that Richard is going to have a long happy life."

"Oh, Bobby," she said. "I hope your right. Where's Teddy? He should be here."

Rebecca who'd been standing near the door, walked over and hugged her Mom.

"Teddy won't come in, Mom," she said. "He blames himself for this."

"But Richard brought Teddy into this."

"I I know Mom, but you know Teddy. He's accepting all the blame. He's going to get better Mom. He has to!!!"

When they all went home that evening, tired and discouraged, they were barely in the door, when a huge black car came down Delaware Drive very slowly, almost stopping as it passed by their door, number twenty-nine.

"It's a warning," said Teddy dully as the car disappeared around the corner. "Their warning us we better not tell who did this to Richard."

"Well, it looks like a big, black hearse," sniffed Rebecca.

"I told you," snapped Bertha. "The bad ones always win."

"All right," said Logania. "They can play their games. The only thing that matters now is for us all to pray for Richard to get well."

Every night, they got together as a family and prayed for Richard's recovery, and like clockwork the black car made it's slow trip past their house every night.

Bertella was even afraid to go to work, but she gathered up her courage and went, and every day, Logania'd sit in Richard's room most of the day and pray over his pale face. That first week, the doctor's would just look sadly at Logania sitting there every day. They'd already told her Richard wasn't going to make it. The second week, she knew them all by name, and had made friends with all of them. Still the doctors offered her no hope, but the nurses would bring her cups of tea and brown bread, as she kept her lonely vigil. In the evening the others would come, but it was the end of the month when Logania first noticed movements in his fingers, then his eyelids would flicker, and finally two months after the accident, Richard opened his eyes. the doctors were amazed for young Richard made a full recovery. The day after Richard returned home, months later, the black car disappeared never to be seen again.

The boys learned a valuable lesson. There is no such thing as easy money, but it was many months before Richard's spirit returned, and laughter echoed in the Mill's house once again.

Richard, having come so close to death, decided it was time now to live. He got a good job, saved his money and eventually bought a house not far from his mother's on Delaware Drive. He met a woman named Lizzie Martin who he immediately fell in love with. It seemed as though he had turned his whole life around. Things went along fine until Lizzie got pregnant, They barely had time to rejoice, because when the baby was born, Richard's beautiful young wife died. Richard grieved for his wife and the tiny infant, whom he named John, became another one of Logania's responsibilities. Logania cared for the young infant until Richard came to realize he loved his son, and could hold him without feeling the resentment he'd built up after his wife's death.

Eventually Richard regained that indomitable spirit of his and taught his young son to enjoy music in the same way he did. Much later in life, Richard even married again, a regal woman by the name of Ardelle and had a daughter named Jael which I had the privilege to baby-sit many times.

CHAPTER 15

Theodore

Theodore was born Oct. 28, 1915, five years after Richard and one year before Robert. Joining the group at school like his brothers and sisters before him, he was the good guy from the start. McCartney School hadn't changed much over the years. Black people were still demoralized and looked down upon. The children of the Mills family suffered much in their pursuit of an education. The double whammy of poverty and dark skin was detrimental to say the least. Young Teddy struggled in the early years of school, but when he reached Jr. High, where sports entered the picture, he excelled.

Football was his favorite, but he was in basketball, baseball, soccer, you name it, Teddy was there. He had many friends. Teddy had such a friendly attitude, it was hard not to like him. Though in every group. there was the one prejudiced child that would yell that hated word nigger, when he was on the field. Most of the class overlooked his color as he bought victory after victory in the between school games. Once you became a friends of Ted's, you were his pal for life.

Once Teddy asked his mother, "why do they call us names all the time, Mom, when they don't even know us?"

"Mostly, Honey, because their minds have been poisoned by their parents, and their parents haven't learned yet that everyone in this world is born equal. We all start out the same, but it's how you live your life that determines your happiness or your sadness.

"But, Mom," responded Teddy. "Look at us. You're the nicest person I know, and you have to struggle so hard. We're so poor."

Logania smiled. I know it seems hard, Teddy, but have you noticed whenever things are at their worst, something happens to resolve the problem, or make things better. That's God doing his work. And when really bad things happen, like Ella's dying, maybe that's a lesson that God is trying to teach us and we just haven't learned it yet."

Teddy just looked at his Mom. He couldn't understand what lesson the death of his sister could teach. He already felt that his mother was a Saint with nothing to learn, but he simply hugged his mother and walked away.

Not many years later, Teddy had to quit school to join his sisters working. He stored up great resentment over this, as he was the Captain of the football team by this time and had a chance to go even farther with a football scholarship, but he never let his mother know the bitterness he stored up over quitting.

Logania though understood. Her strong belief in God is what allowed her to keep going when she knew each of her children resented quitting school.

Teddy's hero, at the time was Hank Aaron, and he'd had dreams of one day being on a major team but those dreams all died when his father defected again, and he was forced to take his father's place as wage earner. His father had once again returned to his family in High Springs, Florida.

Perhaps that was part of the reason he got involved with the gangsters that hung out on Pine St. From Brooklyn to Easton, they came with their schemes and rackets to lure innocent poor children into a life of crime. He and his brother Richard seeking easy money, got into deep trouble, which resulted in his brother Richard being injured almost to the point of death.

Teddy suffered much during the period of time his brother lay near death after the attack on him. When Richard finally recovered, he swore he'd never stray away from the rules his mother taught him ever again. Everyday he worked, never missing a day, trying to erase the guilt, he still felt over his brother Richard.

When he reached age twenty-one, Ted had a circle of loyal friends. Through these friendships, Ted became one of the founding fathers of the Paradise Club. He always did favors for his friends, so it was no surprise when he was elected Secretary Treasurer of the Humanitarians, an organization dedicated to helping the less fortunate. Later in life, he became a lifelong member of both organizations, though Ted's first responsibility was always to provide a home for his mother.

Down at the end of Delaware Drive was an intersection which separated Delaware Drive from Bushkill Drive. A few blocks up this street was Front Street, where the gas plant sat. Huge tanks full, where they stored natural gas for the city's use.

On Oct. 24, 1943, one of the worst disasters Easton ever experienced happened. The Gas Plant blew up at 5.10 on a Sunday morning. Two people died instantly, and one several hours later.

Teddy, hearing the explosion ran from our house on Delaware Drive to the explosion site. What a sight he must've faced. Flames shooting into the sky and the smell of burning gas, and injured people everywhere screaming for help. Despite the heat of the flames as they licked dangerously close to him, Teddy ran into the wreckage and pulled to safety two people who otherwise might have died. The total count of people dead in the blast was three and could've been much higher if it hadn't been for the courageous act of young Teddy and many others who risked their lives. That is the way Teddy lived his life, always helping others, even to the point of risking his own life if necessary. Young Rebecca called Skeeter, who was stationed in Mississippi at the time, to tell him the news of Teddy's bravery and the news of the explosion. This happening right in the middle of World War II, must've been a hard period of time for Logania. In later years, he never missed a foot ball or basketball game and always looked for another athlete in the family and found a couple too. My Uncle Ted, loyal son that he was, looked after his mother her entire life. When Logania passed on, he kept all of the grandchildren in line, being the stern father to all of us, as he never had a child of his own. Freed of the responsibility of his mother, he married long time sweetheart Bealah in a union which lasted twenty-one years. He never grew very tall in stature, but in integrity and love and courage, he was a giant.

—

CHAPTER 16

Rebecca

I have mentioned earlier in this book that Logania's last child was Rebecca. Born March 22, 1921, a joy she was from birth. She arrived when Logania was forty years old, a change of life baby, she was a surprise to all, but was such a delightful baby from the start, it took away some of the sting of the loss of Florence. All the older brothers and sisters loved her and there was never a shortage of baby sitters. What fun to introduce her to the delights of Delaware Drive. Teddy, even when I came along would brag about what a terrific swimmer, Rebecca was when she was taken by her brothers and sisters to the Wilson Dam.

With Bertha, Teddy, and Bertella now working, finances had improved slightly. Rebecca discovered the delights of Heimie's store where with a few cents, she could return home with an enormous supply of dots, candy straws, and licorice sticks.

School for her was a great new adventure. She had the feistiness of Bertha and the creative sensitivity of Bertella and did extremely well in school. McCartney School was still the school, the Mills family went to. It seemed as though March School on College Hill, where Stephen and Skeeter had excelled, was now off limits to blacks. So Rebecca went to McCartney School and suffered the racial slurs and sneers just as her brothers and sisters. One morning Rebecca was called from her desk to the office. Her dad Levi, stood there tall and dynamic.

"Daddy," Rebecca said with a smile. "Are you taking me home?"

"No, Honey, I've come to tell you good bye," said Levi.

"Good bye, but why, Daddy?" asked Rebecca.

"I have to go home and see my family in High Springs, but I'll be back, Honey. So you take care of Mommy, and don't fight with your brothers and sisters. Now walk me to the door."

"All right, Daddy," whispered Rebecca.

At the door as Rebecca watched her father walk away, she felt a sinking feeling in her stomach and she almost ran after him. Instead she returned to class and sat quietly back in her seat.

"Who was that?" asked the teacher.

"My father," answered Rebecca glumly.

"Really, well what did he want?" the teacher asked

"To tell me good bye. He's going to Florida."

"Florida?" "That's pretty far away. Are you sure that's what he said?" Rebecca watched as she winked at the class.

"I guess I know where my Daddy's family lives. He's going to High Springs, Florida. He's been there lots of times," yelled Rebecca angrily.

Then she said nothing else the rest of the afternoon. She had a big lump in her throat like she could cry any minute and she didn't want anyone to see her cry in class. Especially not this teacher. That evening when she was playing with her brothers and sisters, she still had that deep feeling of sadness, which would not go away. Rebecca's premonition was valid, for that day was the last time she saw her father alive. Levi never returned.

Logania received a letter soon after he left, saying that Levi died of Malaria Fever in Florida from his brother and asking where to ship the body. Poor Logania. This time Levi wouldn't be back. After much discussion, it was finally decided that Levi would be buried in Florida with his family and Logania would send the insurance money there. On the day of Levi's funeral, Logania made all the children get cleaned up and sit quietly through the time that Levi was being buried in Florida to show their respect for their father.

After McCartney, Rebecca went on to Taylor. The family was still poor and had to wear hand me downs. So one morning Rebecca had to go to school in a pair of white shoes with one broken heel. A teacher noticed her limping and sent her to the basement to pick a pair of shoes from the discards given to the school for the poorer kids. Rebecca couldn't find any to fit but she did hear two teachers discussing her and her pathetic situation in snobbish tones as she returned to class.

Mom always told her to forgive others when they'd hurt her, but she wondered angrily if things would ever change so people could be respected for who they are, not how rich they were or the color of their skin.

Jr. High years started and still Rebecca remained in school. It was during this time her brother Bobby passed away. It was several weeks before she could concentrate on school work again, and she wondered if they'd ever be free of the bonds of poverty and tragedies. Rebecca persevered and continued in school to Easton High. Yes, the youngest of Logania's children determined to finish school to the end, even taking a College Prep program where she struggled to learn French. Rebecca had dreams of becoming a nurse, but times hadn't changed much. Prejudiced schoolmates thought nothing of passing her in the halls and calling her nigger as they sashayed past. Rebecca, though struggled on.

She was even asked to the Senior Prom by a young man named Harry Draper, but her pride would not let her go in worn shoes and a second hand prom dress.

Though she yearned to be a nurse, she couldn't afford the entrance fee or money for books, so she put that dream to rest, though Rebecca graduated from Easton High School, the first child in Logania's huge family to finish school. The whole family sat in the auditorium as Rebecca Elizabeth Mills received her diploma that night. They weren't the best dressed family there, but they were sure the proudest. How the family celebrated that night. Everyone had to try on her hat and robe and look at her diploma. Though everyone felt a little sad that they weren't the one graduating, they were all very proud of their little sister. In fact everyone had contributed so she could rent her graduation robe. There was plenty of food to eat that night and even some of the neighbors were invited as the Mills family played out some of their favorite skits for Logania.

The social life for blacks in Easton even in 1939 was nil. The only types of jobs for a colored woman was someone's maid, and events held were for whites only. So for Rebecca, a young girl just graduated, her only choices were private parties given by friends. There was one place the young colored people use to hang out called The Century Club. Of course it was for twenty one and over but the younger ones use to sneak in, just to dance to the jukebox and congregate to talk to each other.

One night not long after Rebecca graduated, she was at The Century Club talking to friends when she spotted a light skinned tall handsome man approaching. All her friends were chattering away about this handsome new face, but he came straight to Rebecca and asked her to dance. When they were on the dance floor, he shouted over the music, "you're the prettiest girl here tonight. What's your name?"

"Rebecca Mills," said Rebecca timidly, "but who are you? I've never seen you around here before."

"Mills, your last name is Mills? Do you have a brother named Teddy?"

"Why, yes I do," answered Rebecca.

"Well, you just have to be my girl, then, because I already know your brother and we're good friends."

"How can I be your girl when I don't even know your name?" said Rebecca with a smile.

"My name is Richard, Richard Calloway," he said. "I live in Bethlehem but it looks like I'll be coming to Easton a lot more often."

Rebecca went home that evening and told her sisters all about the amazing man she'd met.

"Oh, oh, looks like our little sister is falling in love," said Bertella.

"No, Honey," said Bertha. "Don't do that. The object is to make them fall in love with you. Then they'll do anything for you."

"Girls," said Logania softly. "Don't tease Rebecca like that."

"Oh, Mom," Rebecca whispered. "He's just perfect. One of the girls at the club offered him a drink and you know what he said. He said, I never drink. It just causes problems."

"Honey, if that's true, then he must be a fine man indeed. You must invite him here to dinner."

It was several weeks before Rebecca saw Richard again, but it didn't take long for them to become a couple. Their favorite hangout became Maddie and Jack's where they'd sit on the front porch and cuddle and kiss and plan their future.

Becky, at eighteen had long wavy, dark hair that hung down her back and bounced when she walked. Her smile was quick to appear and she made everyone feel good around her. She had a vibrant personality which truly sparkled when she was happy. Is it any wonder that Richard fell in love with her? Before Richard came along, Becky had gone out with a few others but found them dull and uninteresting, quite possibly because her own personality made theirs seem lackluster. But, with Richard, everything was different. He was handsome, dynamic, had purpose, and a plan for life that he intended on following.

Now young Richard had an old rattletrap car which he drove to Easton often to visit Rebecca. One night in the old car, their embraces didn't end with kisses and Rebecca knew it was time to plan a wedding.

Rebecca Elizabeth Mills and Richard Calloway were wed on Jan. 8, 1940 in the colored church with both their families and just a few close friends. Everyone rejoiced for the happy couple except Bertha. She'd wanted Rebecca to become a nurse, not just another housewife, working in drudgery for the rest of her life.

""Becky, I know your Richard is handsome, but you're a high school graduate. You have the chance to be something in life."

Becky who was deliriously in love by this time answered, "I am going to be something. I'm going to be Mrs. Richard Calloway."

Bertha just shook her head and hugged her younger sister. She was such a joy in the family, and she had to admit her Richard was a right fine specimen of a man.

They rented a little home on Maple Street right behind the church where they'd married. Richard got a job right away, already working on his plan he'd set up for life. Becky was very happy in her new married life, and close enough to visit Logania whenever she chose. Maybe she too still longed for that nurses career, but in 1940 blacks were still being treated unfairly and she knew her chances, even with money, were slim of ever becoming a nurse.

Soon she had other things to think about, for a baby was on the way. She was so excited. A baby would put the sealing touch on their love. Soon as Richard heard about the baby, he wanted to move to a bigger house, which they did. They found a house on Fifth Street with six rooms and a bath, a miracle house after the other houses Rebecca had lived in. Indeed from time to time Logania, Wesley, and other members of the family would spend the night there.

June 26, 1940, Rebecca delivered her little girl whom she christened Lois Ann. She was a beautiful baby, light skinned with honey colored hair. Rebecca felt blessed. Her love for this sweet little girl and her husband Richard grew in strength every day.

Just two years later, a little boy was born who she named William Marshall Calloway after his grandfather. A perfect family, Richard was so proud of his young wife and their two children, but she started talking about getting a job, he got upset.

"Honey, Becky," would plead, "I know how you feel. But look how much sooner we'll be able to buy a house if we both work."

"Well, Richard," said slowly. "Maybe when both children are in school."

So Rebecca had to be content with that. She took to visiting her mother every day with the kids until one day Richard couldn't find her after work. When he finally located her at Logania's house, he said, "Honey, your married to me now. I would like to see you occasionally when I come home from work."

Soon Lois was old enough to attend school. When it came time to enroll Lois in school, Rebecca was told that Lois would have to attend Taylor School.

"Why does my daughter have to go all the way to Taylor when we live so close to March School," Rebecca asked.

"Mrs. Calloway," answered Mrs. Roberts. "I'm sure it's just because March School attendance records are so high this year."

Rebecca knew that was a lie, but she simply accepted the registration papers and enrolled Lois in Taylor School. When William was also attending school, Rebecca decided it was time to get a job. She walked to 13th and Bushkill because she didn't have enough money to take the trolley. She walked into a company called Seam proof as they had a huge sign on the door WORKERS NEEDED. When Rebecca asked for an application, she was aware of a lot of whispering going on in the background. Carefully she filled out the application so proud she could mark graduate in the slot marked schooling.

"O.K.", said the interviewer, Miss Rackett, we'll let you know. Do you have a phone?'

"No," said Rebecca, "Your sign says you need workers. Why can't you tell me now."

Miss Rackett folded the application nervously, "Mr. Robbis, the big boss isn't in today. He has to O.K. all applications. Do you have an address? We can send you a post card."

"Well, all right," said Rebecca. "How long before you let me know? I'm ready to work now."

"Give it about two weeks," Miss Rackett answered. You'll get a card by then."

When Rebecca disappeared through the door and it slammed shut behind her, she turned to her friend Alice sitting behind her.

"Do you believe that nigger actually expects to get a job here?' she asked.

"It's unbelievable," answered Alice. "There getting so uppity lately. Wanting to work next to white people."

On Rebeccas application, she scrawled in big blue letters COLORED and than threw it in the drawer.

About a month later, Rebecca still hadn't received her post card. Back she went to Seam Proof and asked to see Mr. Robbins. When Mr. Robbins finally appeared, she pointed to the sign still hanging professing, workers needed.

"I applied a whole month ago," she said, and no one sent me a card. Do I have the job or not?"

"Mrs. Calloway, I'll just have to pull your application and see."

After searching the files for five minutes, he called his assistant, Miss Rackett.

"Miss Rackett, where is Mrs. Calloway's application? I can't fmd it in the files."

Sheepishly Miss Rackett reached in her drawer and pulled out Rebecca's application. Rebecca gasped when she saw the blue marks COLORED scrawled across her application.

Mr. Robbins merely picked it up and began reading it carefully. When he finished reading it, he eyed Miss Rackett angrily.

"Why wasn't this shown to me?" he asked.

"Because," gasped Miss Rackett, "you can see for yourself, she's colored."

"Mrs. Calloway," he said, "I apologize for my coworkers here. You seem to have excellent credentials. You can start next Monday."

It wasn't easy working with the others, that whispered and talked about her, and just waited for her to make a mistake, but she stuck it out. A couple of the workers even became close friends with Rebecca and Rebecca stayed with Seam Proof a long time.

As her children grew, she found better jobs and they moved into nicer homes and eventually Rebecca even became a teacher, but she never forgot Mr. Robbins, the one man who'd given her a chance when no one else would because of the color of her skin.

—

In later years, Rebecca helped her mother, Logania, and the rest of the family move next door to her, but she never forgot that first job and the way her heart sank when she saw COLORED scrawled across her application.

CHAPTER 17

Diane Flood

In the year of 1955 while my grandmother, Logania was still recovering from a severe stroke, a new disaster crept over the horizon. It must have been the year for hurricanes hitting the eastern coast.

Starting August 11th, and lasting until the 14th, Hurricane Connie passed by our area and though she'd lost most of her wind power, she drenched the area with her rains. Four days of continuous rain from sodden gray ominous skies.

Several days after, Hurricane Diane followed the same route dropping twenty inches of rain within a two day period. Her slow trek past the Lehigh Valley lasted from August 17th to the 20th. Dams and reservoirs, already overloaded with Connie's contribution broke their bonds and sent tons of water crashing into the Delaware River.

Now when you live next to a river, you keep a careful eye on the amount of rainfall you receive and the level of the water. We watched the river come up to the bridge many times before. It was exciting to watch it rise, exhilarating, and a little bit frightening. But we knew the river always crested before it reached the top of the bridge, so of course that Saturday, when the rains stopped, we were in our usual place watching the water rise. However it rose and rose and continued to rise. Soon we all stood transfixed in fear as we watched it come over the bridge into the street and still keep rising. It wasn't long before we were cut off from crossing the bridge and going uptown or to any of our usual haunts. It moved out into the street slowly creeping up the street, inch by inch like some watery blob. If you've seen the movie, you know what I mean.

We ran home in panic, "Mom, Grammy, the river's in the street and it's still rising!!!"

Mommy went to turn on the radio to hear the news report. It was a beautiful hot summer morning. Nothing bad could happen on such a day.

"Don't worry, Honey," she said to me. "I'm sure it will stop rising soon."

On the radio, the announcer was talking about some darn that busted in the Poconos and a whole boy scout camp destroyed, that had been in its path. This was serious.

Anxiously my Mom called her sister Rebecca, who lived high on a hill, out of the flood area.

Rebecca, immediately wanted her mother, who was still recovering out of the house, away from the danger.

"You all have to come up here, she told my mother, before it gets any higher. We'll have to meet you on College Hill for all the streets leading to Delaware Drive are blocked by water."

We were going to have to walk our Logania up the lane, a hard job for a young person in good health. We younger ones went to check the water again. We didn't have to go far. It had rounded the corner and was creeping up our street, like a green yellowish monster, moving slowly along carrying with it all the trash it had destroyed and dragged on it's way.

"Mom!' I cried in panic. It's right down the street. We have to go!"

My mom was frantically trying to get Logania to come, who really didn't want to leave. She was still straightening this and fixing things which in a few hours would be underwater. Finally Uncle Dick took her arm and led our Logania from the house. We each took some clothes along and began our trek up Delaware Drive to the lane, with the water crawling ominously up the street behind us. If Logania'd lingered any longer the water would've swirled around our front steps, making it impossible for Logania to leave.

Our progress up the lane was slow, as poor Logania had to walk over sticks, rocks and jutting stones, in her house slippers. She never wore anything else. Her one weakness was her sore aching feet.

We finally reached the top of the lane and there was Aunt Rebecca waiting with the car to drive us to her house. Uncle Teddy and several other neighbors from Delaware Drive camped out in the upper yards that night as the muddy black water swirled and climbed and ruined our house. Neighbors helped neighbors as they carried whatever they could to the second floor, not knowing how far the waters would rise.

Safe at Aunt Becky's, we children kept calling the house on the phone as the water continued to rise. When all we heard was a bubbly ring, we knew the phone, too, was under water. The water level reached about to the top of the ceiling on the first floor. Even though Teddy tied the refrigerator down, it floated and banged about and was useless after the flood. Logania's new refrigerator that she'd bought with the money from her Daddy's farm. Ruined.

Later on, when the flood waters receded, the Red Cross came to help, while everyone worked on shoveling out tons of river mud from their homes. To me our street never smelled the same after that. No matter how much hosing the fire companies did, the air in the hot September sun smelled rancid, turning your mind to all the things that died in the water.

We all stayed away about two weeks while the men hosed down and swept mud and dirt for days. The Red Cross kept them supplied with food as they worked and then later supplied us with a new refrigerator and new linoleum's and whatever else was totally ruined. Our Logania was anxious to return to her home, but I after the flood, never felt comfortable in that house again. I would close my eyes to sleep and see that water again creeping slowly up the street, then wake up in a panic. In fact, I spent several days at my father's house until I got my nerves under control.

Perhaps Logania had misgivings about returning also, but if so she kept any complaints to herself. That was the type of person she was. At any rate, her daughter Rebecca went to work on organizing a way to get her mother off Delaware Drive and nearer to her. In the meantime, I remember the never ending battles to keep the floors waxed after that when no matter how much scrubbing my mother did, the black silt left by the water eventually worked its way back to the newly waxed floors.

The next year, my father died, which ended another chapter in my mother's life and mine also. The year after, success, Rebecca had arranged a way we could rent the house next to hers with a beautiful long yard and a real bathroom. I was so thrilled to have my own room, I didn't mind walking miles to finish my Jr. High years.

And Logania, at last in a beautiful house, with all her children nearby, and no money worries for the first time in her life. I think she thoroughly enjoyed this new life, the huge Christmases when all the relatives came, the big Thanksgiving dinners when we'd have to use two tables to seat everyone. To be able to visit her youngest daughter whenever she wanted and a real bathroom, at last. Yes, I think our Logania liked the new house.

CHAPTER 18

Logania's Death

I've already mentioned that Logania suffered a severe stroke in 1955 before the floods came. I still remember how we'd say sentences to her and she repeat everything back twice in that gentle soft voice of hers as she taught her brain to speak again. The whole left side of her body had been affected, but gradually her body relearned everything it had forgotten.

In 1958, Logania suffered another stroke. Her tired worn body, now in its seventy-seventh year could not fight off the effects of the second stroke. Day after day, one or all of her children would go to the hospital and minister to her needs. Turning her body, trying to prevent the endless bed sores, washing her off, trying to feed her, and most of all talking. Talking to her constantly to bring her back to us. Logania was the guiding light for all of us, grandchildren included and we all needed her so.

That summer Uncle Dick (Rebecca's Richard) had planted corn at the bottom of our yard for Logania. Everyone loved her so. Each day Rebecca and Dick would tell her how tall her corn was getting and how she had to come home and see it. We all visited her. How strange to see our Logania, not bustling about getting someone's dinner or putting clean sheets under somebody's head. Still Logania hung on to life until June 26, 1958, Lois's birthday. I believe she didn't ever want us to think of this day as a sad day, so she picked her day to leave this earth so it would never be known as a day of sadness.

Later on that day, surrounded by sky high corn, knee high tomato plants, Uncle Dick stood under a bright, sunny sky and wept for our Logania. Her beautiful corn which she never came home to see. But you know what. I think our Logania did see her corn blowing softly in the wind, on that June day. I think she saw everything that went on after her death and still lends a helping hand whenever we need it.

After Logania's death it was as if we had lost our guiding light. The gloom of the house was so thick you could cut it with a knife. That evening, a huge bat got into my mother's bedroom as if to put the finishing touches on a horrible day.

"Mom, mom," I called, "Come into my room," and I held the door open for her but she was too scared to move. Finally Teddy and Uncle Dick, after much battling, got the horrid thing captured, and took it outside.

The day of Logania's funeral, the sun shone gloriously again making the reason for our coming together seem like a bad dream. Friends and neighbors came from far and near to pay homage to Logania. Our Logania gone to wear her crown of stars, to be with God at last. I'm sure Bobby and Ella were there to greet her and place little Florence in her arms again.

That weekend we young were all confined to the house by Rebecca. The adults were all depressed and heavy doom hung over the house. We younger ones had planned to go to the Sweet Shoppe that night before the worst happened. Unable to stand the gloom of the house, we talked our parents into letting us at least go to our friend's house. Forbidden to go anywhere near the Sweet Shoppe, we all went to our individual friend's house.

At my friend's house, they talked me into going to the Sweet Shoppe. No one will know if you go," they said. "Come on."

So I went, but I felt so guilty, I hid in a dark corner and left within ten minutes, sneaking out like a common criminal, but I was there long enough to see both my cousins William and Lois come in also, look guiltily around and leave right away also. We never told our parents and the time we spent there was as I said less than ten minutes. But my bet is our Logania up in heaven, had a hearty laugh at our expense maybe even a heartier laugh than the wedding gown incident.

CHAPTER 19

Conclusion

Recently they canonized Katherine Drexel, a woman from Philadelphia, daughter of a banker, who at the age of 30 gave away 20 million dollars. A woman who gave away all her millions to found schools for the American Indians and Blacks in the Southwest. She chose poverty, even I hear, eating the scraps off of the other sisters plates and making a folding chair into a wheel chair when she got older. a remarkable woman, I agree.

But my grandmother, Logania, born of a woman who once was a slave grew up in poverty, yet her entire life, she gave of herself, everything she had to give. She gave her time, caring for her family, she gave up her home to go North to earn money for her family, (incidentally Logania never returned to Charlottesville and I know she must've wanted to many times.) After being wed, she gave all of her love to her children and their children. Any stray that happened by her home, she invited in and fed. Many homeless people spent nights sleeping in her cellar and eating of her meager supply of food. And with all the disasters in her life, some listed in this book, the death of three children, one stillborn, one child brutally and deliberately hurt, that lingered near death for months, and the death of her husband, Logania never lost her faith in God.

Then there were the tragedies of the in laws, one of the husbands shot, one of her son's wife dying in childbirth, the death of her other daughter's husband almost at the same time as his child's birth and on and on.

Throughout all this our Logania was a Saint. Soft spoken and gentle, never yelling or complaining, always there to comfort, protect, and love. She was one of the kindest people I have ever known. A true Saint, don't you think, to have no material things to give, but to give so much to so many.

In Logania's twilight years, after suffering a second stroke which she fought to recover from, our Logania at last succumbed and went home to be with God.

She died as her son, Bobby predicted in a beautiful house, with a real bathroom, living with two of her daughters and her son, next door to another daughter surrounded by loving children and grandchildren and even great-grandchildren.

Before her death, year after year, we'd have family reunions for Logania when all the children and grandchildren, and great-grandchildren would come together to honor this wonderful woman. The gifts she passed on to us are dignity, courage, integrity, love for your fellow man, family loyalty, to never give up, and faith in God.

Most of the people in this story are in heaven now. Aunt Bertha, smart and feisty but loving, Uncle Teddy, the loyal son and athlete of the family, who always looked for another in all the future grandchildren, my Mom, Bertella, so sensitive and loving with a talent to make beautiful music and write poetry, Uncle Richard with his gold tooth who could really make those drums hum, Aunt Ella, who loved babies and died of an appendicitis before I was born, Uncle Bobby, with views on life way before his time who died of a goiter, and a first cousin Peter who died tragically by his own hand, and little Florence who died in the womb never seeing the light of day, and my dear sister Marjorie, who found the poem which gave this book it's title, so loving, kind and talented with her wonderful singing voice. Then there are all the in laws that passed on. Their stories would fill another book. But I know they are all in heaven, looking down upon us, giving us a helping hand when we need it, inspiring a little happiness when we are at our saddest, and joining us on the happy occasions in our life and clearly I can hear Grammy Mills saying when things are at their worst, "Remember, Honey, God never puts more on us than we can bear.

In 1977, twenty-one years after Logania's death the family started the three day family reunions in Charlottesville, VA, where all the descendants of the original Armstead family would come to honor their ancestors.

My first cousin Dr. Harry James Ford organized and created the family tree chart which tantalized me into writing the story of Logania. Though I only made it to one of the family reunions, (my children were young then and the reunions were always held the Labor Day weekend right before back to school) I understood in that one instance the reason for them.

To visit that same little church my grandmother went to every Sunday, to follow the same paths she must've traveled with her brothers and sisters, to visit the cemetery where Ardelia and Harry Armstead are buried. It was like traveling back in time and reliving the simple life they must've led.

At one of the reunions, the family traveled to Charlottesville's Court House Square, where the slave auction house still resided. My great grandfather Harry Armstead born 1843 was sold at this site. A sad memory, but also a deep appreciation for our ancestors and their courage which has brought us to the point where we are today. I only remember ever seeing one of my grandmother's sisters, Aunt Bessie from Pittsburgh who came with first cousin Harry Ford Cousin Louise Ford when I was only three. How my grandmother must've missed her family but she never complained.

The cemetery where Ardelia and Harry Armstead are buried

When Harry Armstead, her father died, he gave to each of his children a portion of money from the sale of the farm. Logania'd practice writing her name for hours, so when her check came, She'd be able to sign it. Of course, she used the money to buy things for the house not herself. Her generosity was well known.

As I said when I started this saga I don't claim to know the exact story, but this is my interpretation of what occurred. I tried to keep exact dates and relied mostly on my family's memories. I may have taken some liberty in the beginning of my story because the names on The Family Tree were so tantalizing, but in later years when Logania goes North to work, everything is basically true. There is no doubt that my grandmother was an amazing woman. I just can't resist telling one more story to emphasize her kindness and cleanliness.

One evening my first cousin, William and I were baby sitting my sister Majorie's little boy. He was very spoiled and cried after his mother all the time. Usually she'd have sneak away so he wouldn't see her leaving. At any rate my cousin and I wanted to see the Walt Disney Show on my grandmother's first television set. We had two hours to get the baby to sleep before our show came on. He yinged and he yanged. I walked him and William walked him, back and

Charlottesville Court House Square where the slave auction house resided

forth. We were desperate to get him to sleep. We tried milk, a new diaper, more walking, no go. Finally from sheer exhaustion, we could see his eyes closing. We both rejoiced. There was hope. As he drifted off to sleep, carefully we laid him down on the couch, very carefully. He gave a few cries and slipped back to sleep. We were victorious. We gave each other the Hi Fi.

Then here came Grammy. "That will never do," she said. "That couch is just too dirty for his little head. Everyone sits there."

"All right," we whispered. "We'll put him upstairs on the clean bed."

Carefully we picked him up. It was a major project to get him up those steps without waking him. Every time he made a sound, we shuddered. But we got him on the bed and we made it back downstairs without waking him. Success!!!! And still five minutes till the show.

When the show came on, we were so engrossed in it, we didn't see our grandmother going up the steps. But after just five minutes of the program, we heard those familiar shrieks. We looked at each other in shock and ran up the steps.

The culprit. Our grandmother. She smiled at us, "I just put a clean white pillowcase under his head," she said trying to talk over the noise.

"You laid his head on the dirty bedspread. All the dust lands on that."

Needless to say we didn't see our program that night, and little David cried till his Mom came home despite our walking, feeding, changing, and cajoling and pleading, but the best part is he didn't have to sleep on the dusty bedspread. My grandmother was the best!!!!!!!

The End

REFERENCES

Old Farms (an illustrated guide) John Vince

Before Freedom Came The University Press, The Museum of the Confederacy of Virginia

Urban Life Lina Leuzzi

www.ingramcontent.com/pod-product-compliance
Lightning Source LLC
Chambersburg PA
CBHW031242280526
45784CB00004B/1679